MORAL COURAGE:

Abraham Lincoln,
Mahatmas Gandhi,
Nelson Mandela,
and
Martin Luther King, Jr.

Robert W. Schrier, MD

Copyright © 2012 by B&B Publishers

All rights reserved. No part of this book shall be reproduced, stored in a retrieval system, or transmitted by any means, electronic, mechanical, photocopying, recording, or otherwise, without written permission. Although every precaution has been taken in the preparation of this book, the publisher and author assume no responsibility for errors or omissions.

ISBN-13: 978-1479213085
ISBN-10: 147921308X

Manufactured in the United States of America

To Barbara,

my love and inspiration for over 50 years,

mother of our 5 children,

and grandmother of our 13 grandchildren.

INTRODUCTION

In modern times there have been very few people who have changed the world for the better in a lasting manner. Such men have shared the characteristics of great moral courage in spite of unimaginable adversities. They have faced violence, imprisonment and death in their efforts to bring equality, justice, and freedom to their fellow men. Their backgrounds, culture and religions were varied and their struggles were against different injustices using different weapons.

Abraham Lincoln, and then Martin Luther King Jr. a hundred years later, fought against slavery, racial prejudices, economic and social inequalities suffered by the African-Americans in the United States. They both lost their lives in their fight against these injustices. Lincoln's struggle involved the tragedies and great loss of lives in the Civil War, whereas King's struggles involved political and social nonviolent strategies. Both Lincoln and King were killed by assassins who were racists.

Mahatmas Gandhi was a major voice for nonviolent protests in his battles for freedom against the British Empire and the caste system in India. He was killed by a fellow Hindu. Nelson Mandela was also a freedom fighter who used nonviolent techniques. However, after decades of nonviolent protests with little progress against apartheid oppression, Mandela decided that violence is sometimes needed to achieve freedoms and justice against dictatorial powers. This led to his 27 years of imprisonment in South Africa.

This book is written about these four freedom fighters whose common enemy was injustice and inequality. Lincoln, Gandhi, Mandela and King were remarkable men who made enormous and lasting contributions. Following them through their childhood and adult lives is inspirational, but also enlightening relative to their courage and frailties, their victories and their defeats, and their ultimate lasting impact on the world.

ABRAHAM LINCOLN

February 12, 1809 – April 14, 1865

Abraham Lincoln was born February 12, 1809 in a log cabin in Kentucky. His grandfather had come to Kentucky with Daniel Boone and was killed by Indians while clearing the woods for farming. Lincoln's father, Thomas, was a farmer without any education. Abraham and his father had some things in common - they were both strong and excellent wrestlers and great storytellers. They, however, had major differences and were not close. Abe was always reading books and for this his father mocked him for "fooling himself with education." Abraham's formal education consisted of a total of six months, so he was primarily self-educated.

Cabin in Hardin County, Kentucky where Lincoln lived until he was 7

When Abe was seven years old his family moved to Indiana where his mother, Nancy Lincoln, died two years later of Milk Illness which may have been brucellosis. One year after Nancy's death, Thomas Lincoln married Sarah Bush Lincoln. Sarah loved Abe and his older sister. Sarah was quoted as saying that "Abe disliked physical labor; he went to bed early and rose early to read." He had a great thirst for knowledge.

Thomas Lincoln, Abraham Lincoln's father

Sarah Bush Lincoln, Abraham Lincoln's stepmother

She said, "Abe was a good boy. His mind and mine seemed to run together." When Sarah married Thomas in Indiana she found the Lincoln family living in an unfurnished cabin with dirt floors.

Abe lived with his family in Indiana from age 7 to 21 years and primarily worked as a farmer for his father. When asked once about his childhood, he stated that it was only a story of being poor.

At age 22 Abe had left Indiana and was heading to New Orleans on a flatboat which got stuck on the dam at New Salem, Illinois. The town's people came down to the river bank to watch as Abe struggled with this problem. Among them was a beautiful girl named Ann Rutledge. After returning from New Orleans he decided to settle

Boarding house in New Salem

Store in New Salem shared by Berry and Lincoln

in New Salem. There he boarded in a small house and started a store with a friend named William Berry. Lincoln said that the only result of this venture was "becoming deeper and deeper in debt." He also courted Ann Rutledge during this time in New Salem. The New Salem residents noted his kindness, honesty, and devotion to reading. Sometimes he would be seen walking through town reading a book. It was in New Salem that he became known as Honest Abe. It was also there where he fell deeply in love with Ann Rutledge and was devastated when she died. Ann's sister said that Abe would go to Ann's grave and sit there for hours in silence. Later he courted Mary Owen, who complained about his manners and rejected his offer of marriage. He became depressed and said, "I can never be satisfied with anyone who was block-headed enough to have me."

In New Salem he also began developing his leadership skills and was chosen Captain of the Volunteers in the Black Hawk War. He ran for the State legislature and after an initial defeat he was elected to three consecutive terms. During his time in the State legislature he also studied to become a lawyer. Lincoln also became interested in Shakespeare in New Salem and he has become known as the only American Poet President. Here is some of his poetic language from his first inaugural address,

> "The mystic chords of memory, stretching from every battlefield and patriot grave to every living heart and hearthstone all over this broad land, will yet swell the chorus of the Union, when touched again, as surely they will be, by the better angels of our nature."

After six years in New Salem he obtained his lawyer's license and decided to move to the capitol in Springfield, Illinois and open a law practice. He arrived in Springfield on a borrowed horse and a few clothes in his saddlebag. He went to the country store to purchase some bedding, blankets, and a mattress which the owner, Joshua Speed, told

Joshua Speed

him would cost $17. Abe did not have the money and worried about paying back a loan if his law practice was not a success. Joshua had another idea. He had a double bed on the second floor of the store and offered to share it with Abe. Apparently at that time there was a scarcity of beds so such sharing was not uncommon. The two became lifelong friends and discussed everything with one another from politics to girl friends.

William Herndon,
Lincoln's law partner

Mary Todd

In Springfield Abe met Mary Todd who was aristocratic, well-educated and somewhat acid-tongued – much different from Ann Rutledge. After becoming engaged Mary and Abe broke off their engagement. The reasons were varied but Mary's sister said it was because Mary was flirting with the very famous Stephen Douglas. This led to another period of severe depression for Lincoln. Mary and Abe, however, eventually married in Springfield. Abe went into a law practice with William Herndon who later wrote that Lincoln's marriage to Mary was "loveless" and that his true love was always Ann Rutledge.

Stephen Douglas, one time suitor of Mary Todd, and opponent in debates with Lincoln

In 1846 in Springfield, at 37 years old, Abe ran for the U.S. Congress and was elected. During his time in Congress Lincoln criticized President Polk for aggression which led to the Mexican War. He decided not to run for a second term and returned to law practice in Springfield. During this time he rode the circuit as a lawyer and became known for his storytelling, honesty and fairness. He would encourage his clients to compromise and settle out of court, a service for which he did not charge them. Then, with the repeal of the Missouri Compromise, which had been forged by his hero, Henry Clay of Kentucky, he became interested in politics again. The Missouri

Congressman Lincoln

Compromise had prevented the expansion of slavery to the Western Territory. He then ran unsuccessfully for the U.S. Senate, but during the campaign the famous Lincoln-Douglas debates took place – Lincoln, the Republican antislavery candidate and incumbent Stephen Douglas, the Democratic anti-abolitionist candidate. Since Douglas was nationally known, these debates made Lincoln better known nationally. Lincoln thought that he won these debates against Douglas and therefore had them published.

Seward, 1860 Republican Presidential candidate, later Lincoln's Secretary of State

At the Republican Presidential Convention in Chicago in 1860, Lincoln was proposed by the Illinois contingent as a dark horse candidate. William Seward, who was Governor then Senator from New York, was the second best known American after John Quincy Adams and most considered him the likely Republican candidate. Another strong candidate was Senator Salmon Chase who had been Senator then Governor from Ohio. There were contentious disagreements about these candidates - Seward was against the expansion of slavery, and Chase was unable to obtain uniform support among his Ohio colleagues. Thus, Abraham Lincoln was the compromise Republican candidate and went on to be elected the 16th President of the United States. He replaced

President James Buchanan

Salmon Chase, 1860 Republican Presidential candidate, later Lincoln's Secretary of the Treasury

James Buchanan who, with the looming prospects of secession of Confederate states and civil war, had tried to appease the slaveholders. He stated that he opposed secession, but believed constitutionally that he was unable to prevent it. Lincoln's stance was that it was the President's responsibility to preserve the Union.

When Joshua Speed left Springfield for Kentucky where he inherited his father's slaves, Lincoln had written him that "the U.S. Constitution did not state that all men are created equal except Negroes." They, however, maintained their friendship and Speed advised Lincoln about the border states during the Civil War. Another interesting letter exchange was between Lincoln and an 11 year old girl, Grace Bedell. She advised the President-elect to grow a beard because he had such a thin face. Lincoln accepted her advice and always had a beard during his presidency.

Grace Bedell Billings at a later date than when she received the note written to her from Lincoln as a young girl

Lincoln with a growing beard (upper) and without (lower)

When Lincoln was preparing to leave Springfield for Washington DC his law partner Herndon asked him if he could keep the law office "Lincoln-Herndon" sign up. Lincoln stated, "Let it hang there undisturbed. If I live, I will come back and we will practice together again." This may have been a premonition about his potential assassination.

Edwin Stanton, Secretary of War

Edward Bates, 1860 Republican Presidential candidate, later Lincoln's Attorney General

Lincoln's appointments to his first cabinet are the basis of Doris Kearn Goodwin's recent book about Lincoln entitled, "Team of Rivals." As Secretary of State Lincoln appointed William Seward and they became close friends. He later stated that Lincoln was the "best and wisest man that he ever met." Lincoln appointed Salmon Chase as Secretary of the Treasury. Chase felt Lincoln was too harsh against the South. Chase was responsible for the governmental funding of the Civil War for the Union. He accomplished this by raising taxes, decreasing government salaries by 10%, printing more money, and selling government bonds. In the 1864 election, Chase, while still in Lincoln's cabinet, encouraged a draft of himself as the Republican candidate rather than Lincoln. Lincoln eventually had to remove Chase as Secretary of the Treasury, but as characteristic of Lincoln's magnanimity, two months later he appointed Chase as Chief Justice on the Supreme Court. Chase was enormously impressed and appreciative. Edwin Stanton was appointed Secretary of War by Lincoln. He had a bearish, intimidating personality. He suffered from asthma and counterbalanced Lincoln's gentle tempered personality. Lincoln and Stanton orchestrated the government's role in the Civil War. Edward Bates was another Republican candidate for the nomination in Chicago who Lincoln appointed to his Cabinet as Attorney General.

With the attack on the Union at Fort Sumter, South Carolina, Lincoln asked Robert E. Lee to head the Union Army. At that time, Lee was superintendent of West Point and was against secession, but he rejected Lincoln's offer, indicating that he could not fight against fellow Virginians. He then accepted command of the Confederate Army. Lee was a brilliant military strategist who early in the Civil War was quite successful, winning the Battle of Bull Run.

Robert E. Lee

President Abraham Lincoln

The penetration of his Confederate Army into Maryland threatened Washington DC. Lincoln had resisted declaring freedom for Southern slaves. However, he cited an agreement with God that if the Union Army won the Battle of Antietam in Maryland, he would announce the Emancipation Proclamation, which he had already written. Thus, in 1862, with the Union victory at Antietam, Lincoln's declaration freeing the slaves in the Confederate states was announced to his cabinet and the nation. At that time there were 250,000 slaves in the Confederate Army.

Lincoln was disappointed with General George McClellan as Commander of the Army of the Potomac for not pursuing aggressively Lee's army after the Antietam victory. Lincoln eventually removed McClellan and later appointed Ulysses Grant as Commander of the Army of the Potomac. Grant's aggressive pursuit of the Civil War has received substantial credit for the Union victory by historians. The Civil War ended up costing 620,000 deaths which, based on the current United States population, would be equal to approximately 6 million deaths. There were more deaths in the Civil War

General George McClellan, Commander of the Army of the Potomac

than World War I, World War II, Korea, Viet Nam, Iraq, and Afghanistan combined. At the Battle of Gettysburg over 7,000 Union and Confederate soldiers died.

At the dedication of the cemetery at Gettysburg the first speaker spoke for two hours, then Lincoln followed with the following words:

It is rather for us to be here dedicated to the great task remaining before us – that from these honored dead we take increased devotion to that cause for this they gave the last full measure of devotion that we here highly resolve that these have not died in vain – that this nation, under God, shall have a new birth of freedom – and that government of the people, by the people, for the people, shall not perish from the earth.

The first speech was not memorable, but Lincoln's words have become immortalized.

Mary Lincoln entered the White House with considerable enthusiasm. She was, however, criticized for her spending, such as purchasing lovely, but expensive, dresses. The Lincolns had lost a child, Eddie, at age 4, and then came the death of William Wallace Lincoln which devastated both parents. Mary subsequently would only wear black clothes in mourning and continued to be depressed.

General Ulysses S. Grant, Commander of the Army of the Potomac

William Wallace Lincoln

Mary Todd Lincoln in mourning for Willie (left) and Mary's dresses

Lincoln felt that he was going to lose his 1864 reelection. There was much resistance against him, not only in the South, but also in the North because of the length of the war and his emancipation policy. Lincoln was the Republican candidate and George McClellan was running against him on the Democratic ticket. Just before the election, however, General William Tecumseh Sherman captured Atlanta and General Philip Sheridan was victorious in the Shenandoah Valley. On this background, Abraham Lincoln was reelected as President. With Grant's capture of Richmond and Lee's surrender at Appomattox, the Civil War was virtually over. Lincoln signed the 13th Amendment to the Constitution which freed all slaves. The 14th Amendment overturned the Dred Scott decision by the Supreme Court and made the former slaves US citizens, while the 15th Amendment outlawed any race-related restrictions on voting.

Abraham Lincoln reelected President in 1864

General William Tecumseh Sherman

Clara Barton

Frederick Douglas

During the Civil War Clara Barton, a former teacher and patent officer, organized a group of nurses to care for the injured soldiers at Bull Run. She became known as the Angel of the Battlefield and founded the American Red Cross. She was supported by Lincoln in her effort to search for missing prisoners of war.

During the War, President Lincoln became friends with Frederick Douglas, a former slave and abolitionist. He was the first black man to dine with a President in the White House. Douglas stated of Lincoln, "He was one of the few Americans who could entertain a Negro without in otherwise reminding him of the unpopularity of his color." He, however, did not resist criticizing Lincoln when he failed to retaliate for the slaughter of black troops in 1864 by the Confederate Army. Nevertheless, he praised his famous friend as "one of the best men that presided over the destiny of this or any country." After Lincoln's assassination, Mary Lincoln gave Douglas Lincoln's antler-head cane in remembrance of their friendship. When Douglas' wife, Anna, died after 40 years of marriage, Douglas was criticized for marrying his white secretary. In response, Douglas stated, "I have supported the rights of colored people not because I am a Negro but because I am a man."

Harriet Tubman was the daughter of a slave who escaped to the North. She is known as the Moses of her people, because of organizing the Underground Railroad for fugitive slaves fleeing to the North. She was an outspoken critic of Lincoln, disdaining his views in colonization which proposed sending freed American blacks to Africa, the Caribbean, or Latin America. She also criticized him for his caution on emancipation and wrote to him, "God won't let Master Lincoln defeat the South until he does the right thing." During the War she was a scout and nurse. She knew Mary Lincoln but never met Abraham Lincoln.

Harriet Tubman (right, and far left in group picture)

Sojourner Truth was another black abolitionist. She was uneducated but became known for being very outspoken against slavery. When there was an attempt to keep her from speaking at a feminist convention, she made the famous statement "Ain't I a woman?" Once she visited Harriet Beecher Stowe, who wrote the antislavery book "Uncle Tom's Cabin," and was so impressed that she wrote about Sojourner in a national magazine.

With Lincoln's Emancipation Proclamation she traveled from Michigan to Washington DC to meet him. Afterwards she stated, "I was never treated by anyone with more kindness and cordiality than was shown by this great and good man Abraham Lincoln." Douglas called her a "strange compound of wit and wisdom, of wild enthusiasm and flint-like common sense."

Painting of Sojourner Truth and President Lincoln

Lee's surrender was the most dangerous time for Lincoln because of the desperation of the Confederacy. He, however, never seemed to care about his safety. For example, during the War he would walk daily unprotected, against his wife's and other's advice, to the nearby War Department to read the ticker tape on the progress of the War. On his return journey to the White House he was not allowed to be alone and was accompanied by soldiers.

On the night of the play, April 14, 1865, the Grants were invited but decided not to accompany the Lincolns to Ford Theater. Lincoln was discouraged from attending the play by Secretary of War Edwin Stanton. His friend and bodyguard, Ward Hill Lamon, always was extremely worried about Lincoln's safety. In fact, not having faith in Lincoln's body guards, he began sleeping outside Lincoln's room at the White House. He personally carried an arsenal of pistols and Bowie knives.

Ward Hill Lamon

Charles Forbes   William Crook

Unfortunately, Lamon was out of town on the night of the assassination, something for which he never forgave himself. William Crook was a White House guard whom Lincoln always bid a good night. On the night of the assassination, however, this did not happen. Crook offered to accompany Lincoln to the play but Lincoln told Crook that he had been on duty all day and needed to go home and rest. Charles Forbes was Lincoln's White House messenger and carriage footman whom Lincoln invited to the play at Ford Theater. When Booth approached Lincoln's presidential box, Forbes stopped him. Booth displayed a card that seemed to authorize his presence and Forbes therefore unfortunately let him pass. Forbes was forever haunted by this mistake. He was a devoted friend and after the assassination

John Wilkes Booth, Mastermind of the Plot, was to kill President Lincoln

moved to Chicago to be near Mary Lincoln who had moved there.

John Wilkes Booth an actor and anti-abolitionist, with other conspirators, planned to kidnap Lincoln and trade him for release of Confederate soldiers. However, when Lincoln spoke from the White House after Lee's surrender, Booth was in the audience. For the first time, Lincoln spoke of black suffrage – i.e., allowing blacks to vote. Booth was outraged and decided then that Lincoln must be assassinated. He and his fellow conspirators met several times at the house of Mary Surratt, a Southern

Major Henry Rathbone

Lewis Powell, alias Payne who was to kill William Seward, Secretary of State

George Atzerodt, who was to kill Vice President Andrew Johnson

Ed Spangler

David Herold

Mary Surratt

Dr. Samuel Mudd

Samuel Arnold

Artist's rendition of Booth at Ford Theater the night of the assassination

Michael O'Laughlin

sympathizer. Booth was to kill both Lincoln and Grant when they were expected to attend a play at Ford Theater. Lewis Powell (alias Payne) was to kill the Secretary of State, William Seward, and George Atzerodt was to kill Vice-President Andrew Johnson. After Booth fired point blank into Lincoln's head, he slashed Major Henry Rathbone, who had been invited with his fiancée to accompany the Lincolns to the play. Booth then jumped from the Presidential box to the stage where another conspirator and stage carpenter, Ed Spangler, had arranged the set for Booth's escape to the alley where another conspirator,

David Herold, had horses waiting. The two rode first to Mary Surratt's house to obtain rifles, ammunition and whiskey. They then went to the house of Dr. Samuel Mudd who put a splint on Booth's leg which was broken during his jump to the Ford Theater stage. Stanton had sent the US Calvary after Booth and they finally cornered him and Herold in a tobacco barn in Bowling Green, Virginia. Booth told David Herold to surrender, but he personally would not.

Secretary of State Seward with scars from the assassins' attack

The barn was set on fire and during the barn burning Booth was shot in the neck and eventually died from the wound. After a jury trial, Surratt was convicted. She was hanged and this was the first capital punishment in the country against a woman. Herold, Powell (alias Payne) who attacked Secretary of State Seward and Atzerodt, who was supposed to kill

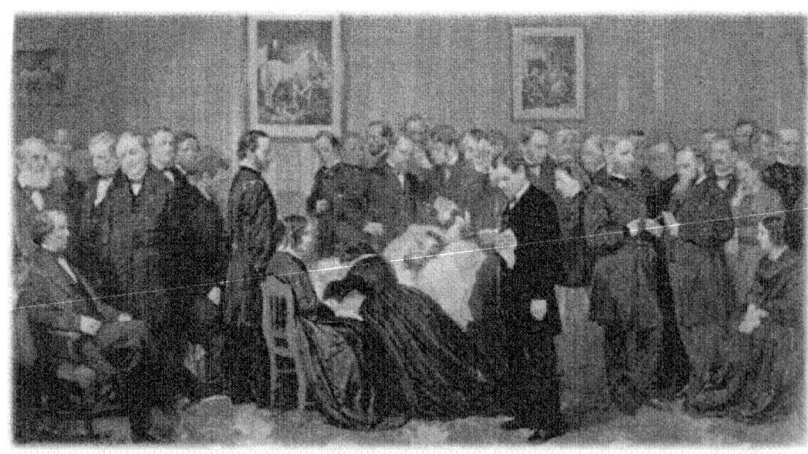

Painting by Chappel of Lincoln's Deathbed and Robert Lincoln at his father's deathbed (right)

Vice-President Johnson but lost his nerve, also were hanged. Samuel Mudd, Ed Spangler, and Samuel Arnold were given life sentences but were pardoned by President Johnson on the eve of Ulysses Grant's inauguration except Michael O'Laughlin, who had died while in prison.

The hanging of the conspirators (left to right) Mary Surratt, Lewis Powell, David Herold, George Atzerodt

From the Ford Theater, the mortally wounded Lincoln was taken to the nearby Petersen boarding house in an unconscious and agonal state. Secretary of War Stanton, rather than Vice-President Johnson, took over the government, believing the assassination to be a Confederate military act. Lincoln's cabinet, Mary and Robert Lincoln, and many others surrounded his bed during his final hours on Good Friday, April 14, 1865.

Ford Theater and rocking chair in which Lincoln was assassinated

The return of Lincoln's body to Springfield took 12 days and in each city there were thousands in mourning. Thousands paid tribute to the slain President during the stop in New York City. Six year old Theodore Roosevelt was in attendance and he idolized Lincoln his entire life. In the South, there was mourning from the thousands of blacks but most whites considered Lincoln a mortal enemy. In the North, millions attended Easter church services which were held two days after Lincoln's assassination on Good Friday. Lincoln was the first non-Jew for whom Kaddish prayers were chanted in synagogues. In Springfield, the town's leaders had purchased six acres in the city center for Lincoln's burial mausoleum, but Mary Lincoln insisted that he be buried outside of the town at the more secluded Oak Ridge Cemetery. She thought that her husband would have approved this quieter site.

Young Theodore Roosevelt (top)

Funeral procession in New York City (right)

Oak Ridge Cemetery

The Lincolns' home in Springfield, at his funeral, with Abe Lincoln's favorite horse, Old Bob

President Andrew Johnson

After his inauguration, during which he was intoxicated, Andrew Johnson initially seemed to project support for Reconstruction of the South with protection of the blacks and he arrested Jefferson Davis, President of the Confederacy. Johnson was, however, from the seceded state of Tennessee and was the sole Senator from the Confederacy who supported the Union. He had replaced Vice-President Hannibal Hamlin from Maine on Lincoln's 1864 reelection ticket. However, after his initial act of arresting Davis, Johnson allowed Southern states to rejoin the Union by only pledging allegiance and recognizing the end of slavery with very little Federal oversight. He primarily supported states' rights, issued widespread amnesty and in essence removed the North from the Reconstruction of the Southern States. President Johnson vetoed civil rights legislation and approved "Black Codes" which limited the freedom of former slaves. He wrote, "This is a country for white men and, by God, as long as I am president, it shall be a government for white men." The result was a failed Reconstruction which led to strict segregation and continued oppression of blacks. Frederick Douglas once led a delegation of freedmen to meet with Johnson about blacks' right to vote. Johnson had little sympathy for the plight of the former slaves and felt that throwing blacks and whites together at the ballot box would lead to "race war". Congress impeached Johnson for aiding and abetting Southern racism, abusing Presidential veto and pardoning power, as well as making a cabinet appointment without Congress approval. The impeachment vote was 32 to 19, missing by one vote the necessary two-thirds to remove Johnson from the Presidency.

In 1866 the secret organization of the Ku Klux Klan was founded in Tennessee to insure white supremacy. The Klan was not only anti-black, but anti-Catholic and anti-Jew. It was headed by former military officers of the Confederacy. They wore white hoods to represent the ghosts of dead Confederate soldiers. They were openly defiant to the Emancipation Proclamation and against increased rights for blacks. They would intimidate and even kill blacks who even considered registering to vote, a freedom supposedly assured by the 15th Amendment.

Ku Klux Klan Member

During this failed Reconstruction period in the South, 3700 lynchings of blacks were reported. Frederick Douglas and others criticized the North about doing nothing about this lawlessness. He said, "If Lincoln were alive we would not hear from the Capitol that there is no power under the Constitution to protect the lives and liberties of American citizens in our Southern states from barbarous, inhuman, and lawless violence." A group of blacks donated funds to commission the Freedman's statue honoring the emancipating Lincoln. On seeing the standing Lincoln with the freed slave kneeling beside him, Douglas said that the black figure should have been portrayed in a more manly position. The kneeling figure was from a picture of the last fugitive slave captured in Missouri.

Freedman Statue   Elizabeth Keckley – "Lizzie"

After her husband's assassination, Mary Lincoln's tragic life continued. Congress felt Mary was not due a pension, which was given to deceased military widows, because Lincoln was a citizen, not a soldier. She was mocked by the press for trying to sell her White House wardrobe to make money. She also was distraught when Herndon told the story about Ann Rutledge, which she had never heard before. Also, her close friend and seamstress, Elizabeth Keckley wrote a book, "Behind the Scenes: 30 years as a slave and 4 years in the White House." In the book, the content of confidential letters between Mary and Elizabeth were included with details such as the people in Lincoln's government whom Mary detested, Mary's out of control spending, and letters threatening her husband's assassination. This devastated Mary because she was so close to Lizzie. For example, during one six week period after the assassination she had written her 16 letters. After these disappointments, Mary then decided to leave the country and went with her son Tad to Germany. In Chicago after the assassination, Tad

President Ulysses S. Grant

Mary Todd Lincoln with an apparition of her husband

had been sleeping with his mother, not allowed to attend school, and at age 14 couldn't write. In Europe he was allowed to attend school and there his education progressed. While in Germany, Congress voted a pension for Mary which President Grant signed. Subsequently, she and Tad returned to the United States. Another tragedy then struck when Tad died, probably of pulmonary tuberculosis. So at the Oak Ridge Cemetery Eddie, Willie, Tad and President Lincoln had been laid to rest. Mary then went into exile again, this time to France at a health spa in the Pyrenees. On her return to the United States, her remaining son, Robert Lincoln, took her to court where she was declared insane. However, her lawyer apparently had an agreement with Robert. After several months in the insane asylum, she obtained another lawyer, was declared sane and released. She never forgave Robert.

Of the four Lincoln boys, Robert was the only one to survive and he became a prominent lawyer. President James Garfield appointed him Secretary of War in his cabinet. He was with Garfield as they were traveling to Williams College for a commencement address when a crazed anarchist shot the President who ultimately died of the complications of the assassination attempt. Equally ironic, Robert had continued to support the Republican Party and was traveling to meet President McKinley when he was assassinated. After being close to three presidential assassinations, Robert felt cursed and decided to completely leave politics. He then became President of Pullman Cars which at that time had segregated train cars. Black leaders, including

Booker T. Washington

WEB Dubois

Booker T. Washington and WEB Dubois, co-founder of the NAACP, requested to meet with Robert Lincoln to discuss the desegregation of trains. The proposed meeting with Abraham Lincoln's son to abolish segregation of trains never occurred. Booker T. Washington had stated about Robert Lincoln's father, "Abraham Lincoln had found (me) as a piece of property and left (me) as an American citizen." He was the second black to dine in the White House with a US President, namely Theodore Roosevelt. Dubois was accused of being a Communist by Joe McCarthy and at age 93 moved to Ghana.

After Lincoln's assassination, many of his admirers wrote books but the most extensive was by his secretarial assistants, John Nicolay and John Hay which was a ten volume book, "Abraham Lincoln: A History," which took over 16 years to write. John Hay had a very distinguished career after Lincoln's assassination. He became Secretary of State for President Grant. Nevertheless, he stated, "The greatest prize of my life was my friendship with Abraham Lincoln."

John Nicolay, Abraham Lincoln, and John Hay

Of note, President Barack Obama was the first to take his oath of office on the Lincoln Bible.

Second Inaugural Address, March 4, 1865, ended with these words:

With malice toward none; with charity for all; with firmness in the right, as God gives us to see the right, let us strive on to finish the work we are in; to bind up the nation's wounds; to care for him who shall have borne the battle, and for his widow and his orphan—to do all which may achieve and cherish a just and lasting peace, among ourselves, and with all nations.

The first Reconstruction may not have failed had Lincoln lived. The Second Reconstruction did not really occur until 100 years later. This was associated in 1964-5 with Lyndon Johnson signing the Civil Rights and Voting Rights Bill. Laws alone would, however, have been inadequate and the Civil Rights movement headed by Martin Luther King, whose 80th birthday was just recently celebrated, was critical in the supporting rights of black Americans. King in 1968 stated that the US might actually have a black President in 40 years, i.e. 2008, the year Barack Obama was elected.

Abraham Lincoln's life has been an inspiration to millions of people worldwide for his courage, integrity, fairness, tolerance, humanity, and commitment to equality during the country's most difficult Civil War times.

Lincoln, Obama, and King

Mohandas Karamchand Gandhi

October 2, 1869 - January 30, 1948

Mohandas Karamchand Gandhi was born on October 2, 1869 in Porbandar, a small coastal city by the Arabian Sea in India. At that time the India of the British Raj contained 500 princely states. Porbandar was on the Kathiawar peninsula whose princely states were ruled by a British agent in Rajkot, a city 120 miles inland. Gujarati was the language of the

Gandhi's birthplace at Porbandar

Gandhi at age 7

Kathiawar region. Mohandas' forbearers had served as administrators for the Katthiawar princes for five generations. Ota Gandhi, Mohandas' grandfather, was the most successful. He was made a first minister (diwan) of the Porbandar territory in which the city of same name resided. Karamchand, also known as Kaba, was Ota Gandhi's son. He was Mohandas' father and he also became a diwan. The majority of

Indians in the region were Hindus with a minority being Muslim. The Hindu caste system was integral to society with Brahmins and then Kshatriya as being the highest castes. The next caste was the Vanias (Banias) to which the Gandhis belonged. The Gandhis considered themselves as a high caste in contrast to the lower untouchable castes. Putlibai was Kaba's fourth wife and the mother of Mohandas. Kaba's first two wives died in childbirth and the third wife also died at a young age. During his early years of life Mohandas (Mohan) lived in a large house with an extended family in Porbandar. Then Putlibai moved her children to Rajkot where Kaba had been made a diwan or ruler. In Rajkot, at age seven, Mohan went to a primary school then to a suburban school. At age eleven Mohan passed his entrance examination to enroll in Rajkot's Alfred High school where English was the language of instruction. He was ninth of seventy boys who took the test. Mohan Gandhi envied the Brahmin caste boys who were identified by their carrying keys on their sacred shoulder to waist dress. As a Banian caste Mohan decided to flaunt a bunch of kemp, which he did not need, on his clothes. In his teenage years he had enthusiasm for the English schools, but also felt the humiliation about the political dominance in India of the English. Although Kaba was a dedicated Hindu and attended the Rama and Krishna temples, Muslims, Zoroastrians, Jain monks and Hindus from the rival Shiva temple visited their home and discussed their respective religions. Mohan was very impressed with his father's open mindedness. His mother was also quite religious and frequently fasted, but also was quite tolerant.

However Putlibai told her children not to touch the untouchable boy Uka who had cleaned their lavatories. If there was an accidental touch of Uka, Mohan would need to bathe to remove the unholy touch. This practice was also to apply to Muslims. Twelve year old Mohan had difficulty in accepting the reason for these rules. Kaba told the children that eating or touching meat was unacceptable for Hindus. Mohan was told that a medical career was not possible for him, because of the need to touch and dissect animals. Smoking and alcohol were also forbidden. Like other high caste Hindu boys, Mohan wore his hair in a knot at the back of his head, a so-called shikha. Nevertheless, Mohan and his older brother, Karsan, smoked cigarette butts thrown away by their uncle. Although parental control was frustrating for Mohan, overall he was quite obedient.

As a 12 year old boy Mohan was haunted by the story of

Harishchandra who clung to truth even at his own expense. At Alfred High School he had Hindu, Muslim, Parsi and other non-Hindu teachers. With his schooling in English and no one in his family knowing English he became somewhat separated from others in his family. In 1882 when Mohan was not quite 13 years old, he was married to Kasturba Makanji Kapadia, a Porbandar girl a few months older than him. His brother Karsan and a cousin were also married at the same time; the triple wedding took place in Porbandar. Although Mohan enjoyed the wedding festivities, he later blamed his father for the "child marriage" which cost him a year of school. The marriage had its problems; three of their first five years of marriage Kasturba lived with her mother.

Gandhi and Kasturba, 1902

Mohan desired the beautiful, uneducated Bania caste girl, but she resisted and was quite independent.

As a child Mohan had fears of ghosts, robbers, serpents and thieves. He would not go out at night and had to always sleep with a light near him. Another boyhood conflict for Mohan was a Muslim boy, Sheikh Mehtab, who was three to four years older than Mohan. He was a friend and classmate of Mohan's brother Karsan. Mehtab was a gifted athlete with great strength, speed and endurance. This contrasted with Mohan, who was very unathletic, did not play sports and often skipped school to care for his increasingly sick father. Mehtab for some reason focused on Mohan and said that he should partake of wine and meat, which were forbidden for religious Hindus. Mehtab told Mohan that eating meat would make him stronger, remove his fears and better control his wife Kasturba's independence. Mohan's brother, Karsan, agreed with Mehtab and indeed was eating meat. Finally Mohan was convinced that eating meat would make Indians stronger and allow them to obtain their freedom from the English. At age 14 Mohan began to relish meat dishes away from home, but after about 12 months of this meat eating phase of his young life, he decided not to further lie to his parents and stopped eating meat. He, however, never told his parents about his meat eating. On another occasion when Karsan was in debt, Mohan clipped a bit of metal off Karsan's solid gold amulet to help Karsan pay his debt. His conscience again prevailed and he felt that he must tell his parents about this theft of gold. He wept as he gave his father his written confession.

When Mohan Gandhi was 16 years old, Kasturba became pregnant. One evening Kaba's brother, Tulsidas, agreed to relieve Mohan from massaging his father's legs so that he could spend time with his pregnant wife. Shortly thereafter, however, Tulsidas knocked on their door and told Mohan that his father had died. Mohan felt guilty that his father did not die in his arms. Kasturba's firstborn died within a few days after birth. Some have said that these events influenced Gandhi's future attitude about sex. Mohan tried unsuccessfully to educate Kasturba. Although not reciprocated, he had a passion for her which included, but was beyond, a sexual attraction. Although Putlibai, Mohan's mother, and his older brother, Laxmidas, felt that Mehtab corrupted Mohan, their relationship continued. Mehtab even convinced Mohan to go to a brothel to prove his manliness and make him more attractive to Kasturba. On seeing the designated women on her bed, Mohan froze and left.

Though Mohan later described himself as a shy mediocre student, that was not really the case. In 1887 he passed his matriculation and was 404th of 3,000 taking the examination in western India. After a term in Somaldas College in Bhavnagar, it was decided that to restore the family's prestige, Mohan Gandhi should go to London. He wanted to study medicine in London, but Laxmidas reminded him that their deceased father would not have approved and wanted Mohan to study for the bar. Mohan was very excited about the prospect of London, but had difficulty finding the necessary financial support. At his mother's request, Mohan Gandhi took a vow that while in London, he would not touch women, wine or meat. In the meantime Kasturba had their son, Harilal, in the spring of 1988. According to Hindu and Indian custom, Kasturba was not involved in her husband's plans to travel to London. His trip to London started in Bombay with Laxmidas who was now head of their family and carried the money for Mohan's trip. Laxmidas left the money with Kasturba's brother and returned to Rajkot. The Banias of Bombay felt that no one of their caste should travel to London and live with the impure whites, so Mohan was jeered in Bombay. He was called before a meeting of the Hindu Bania caste and told that it was against their religion for anyone in their caste to travel to London. Mohan disagreed and stated that he did not believe that his traveling to London was against his Hindu religion. The Hindu head of the meeting therefore told Mohan that he would be an outcast. Moreover, Kasturba's brother would not release the necessary funds to Mohan for the trip. Mohan therefore had to obtain a loan for his passage which Kasturba's brother would have to repay. Thus, on September 1988, the now strong and obstinate Mohan Gandhi sailed from Bombay on the Clyde liner enroute to London. The trip was not easy for Mohan, particularly since as a non-meat eater he had to survive on sweets and fruits. On September 29, 1988 the Clyde docked in Tilbury, then Mohan took a train to London. After a few days in hotels Mohan moved into an English home in Richmond with a Brahmin Kathiawarin, Dalpatram Shukla. He had just turned nineteen years old, and was terribly homesick for his mother, wife, and son. He would cry himself to sleep. Shukla urged Mohan, who was now being called Mohandras, to read British daily newspapers. This helped his English and exposed him to politics. Shukla also tried unsuccessfully to have Mohandras break his vegetarian vow. Mohandras began his three year legal studies in London.

They required mostly personal study with few classes and lectures. To pass the bar two sets of examinations needed to be passed, one in Roman law and another in common law. There were also six dinners a term, and there were twelve terms over the three years. During one of Mohandras long walks (8-10 miles/day) to his great joy he came across a vegetarian restaurant named The Central. He also bought and read Henry Salt's "Plea for Vegetarianism." This led him to become a vegetarian by choice not by vow. In order to become a proper Englishman he took lessons in dancing, violin, French and elocution. This infatuation, however, lasted only three months. He realized that what he needed was not a way to impress others but steadfastness in seeking goals. He also relished a desire to reflect and write. What remained during this time of self-reflection was his English fashion clothes including a top hat. Another aspect to Mohandras London life was passing himself off with young ladies as a bachelor, because of his embarrassment about his childhood marriage. On one occasion, however, a young woman friend appeared to become serious. He therefore wrote her a letter revealing that he was married.

In June 1880 Mohandras passed his matriculation examination. Before his bar finals in December 1890 he was very involved in the vegetarian movement and was elected to executive committee of the London Vegetarian Society. He was also considering whether he should become an atheist or follow a particular religion. He purchased and read the Bible and attended many services by Christian ministers. He also went to Muslim meetings and had Muslim friends. Mohandras, however, remained tentatively loyal to Hinduism which seemed more tolerant of other religions and did not claim to be the sole possessor of truth.

From December 15 to 20, 1890, Mohandras took and passed the bar finals. He then only had twelve more dinners to pay for and attend. He was a favorite for the tables of four at the dinners. This was because he didn't drink alcohol, so the two bottles of port or sherry at the table could be consumed by the other three persons. During his free time before attending his final dinners Mohandras wrote several articles for the Vegetarian Magazine, and also gave talks and interviews about being a vegetarian. He also talked about The Foods of India. While initially these activities were non-political, they progressed whereby he felt that vegetarians were more likely to be sympathetic to the aspirations and rights of Indians.

After becoming a barrister, Mohandras left London as a much more sophisticated, but still shy individual. He wondered how his Bania caste back home would accept him. After a rough sea voyage, he was met in Bombay by his brother, Laximdas, with bad news. Their mother, Putlibai, after hearing her son had passed his final bar exam, died at the age of 41 years. Mohandras had not had an opportunity to tell her that in England he had kept his vows regarding no meat, wine, or women. On his return to India he went through a cleansing ritual in an attempt to bond again with his Bania caste community. However, detractors of his age group were not appeased and wanted him to pay a fine, which he refused. The parents of Kasturba belonged to this minority group and they were not allowed to even offer Mohandras a glass of water in their home. He again tried to educate Kasturba, who could not read, but as with his previous attempts before London, he failed. He, however, was much more successful in bonding with his three year old son, Harilal. Later however Kasturba became receptive and their relationship improved. In October 1892 their second son, Manilal, was born. Mohandras had a difficult time starting a law practice in Rajkot and had no better fortune in Bombay. Moreover, he had an encounter with the British

Raj's political agent in Kathiawar which he felt depicted white racial arrogance. Gandhi was enraged and he lost his desire to practice law in Rajkot. He then was offered a position by a firm, the Dada Abdullah and Co., which was pursuing a lawsuit about a large claim in South Africa. Mohandras was offered first class roundtrip fare to South Africa and a remuneration which would allow him to repay his brother for the financial support that he had received while in Great Britain. Thus on April 19, 1893, Mohandras left Bombay by ship for Durban, Natal in South Africa. When he landed in Durban he wore a black turban, striped trousers, a frock coat, tie, a watch and chain, looking like a very sophisticated Anglicized barrister. Mohandras, however, sensed a smugness and arrogance of the white South Afrikaners towards Indians. The owner of the firm, Abdullah, had amassed a fortune by selling South African gold to India. He now owned several ships and businesses. At first Abdullah was put off by this fancy dressed lawyer from India, but later he became

Gandhi in his English fashion clothes

impressed with the capabilities of Mohandras. In his first court appearance Gandhi was asked to remove his turban. He felt that this was an act of humiliation, so he refused and walked out of the court. Abdullah's case requesting 40,000 British pounds was being held in Pretoria, the capital of Transvaal. So Gandhi left for Pretoria where racial discrimination against Indians was worse than in Natal. Indians right to own land and to trade in Transvaal were markedly restricted. Although Gandhi had a first class ticket to Pretoria, as an Indian he was forced by the police to travel third class. Nevertheless, Gandhi was successful with the case by negotiating a settlement out of court which favored Abdullah. Evidence of racism against not only Indians, but also blacks and colored, was continually observed by Gandhi. Once he was walking on a sidewalk close to the modest home of the Transvaal President, Paul Kruger, and a guard pushed and kicked him into the street. He also needed a letter from a white Afrikaner barrister to allow him to go out after 9:00 pm in Pretoria.

In South Africa Gandhi had close friends who tried to make him a Christian. He said, however, that he could not believe that Jesus was the only incarnate Son of God. Gandhi was, however, overwhelmed by the Sermon on the Mount and Leo Tolstoy's writings. Tolstoy chose five commandments from the Sermon on the Mount including do not hate, do not lust, do not hoard, do not kill, and love your enemies. Thus began Gandhi's turning away from violence and beginning devotion to nonviolence (satyagraha). At the same time he read a translation of the Islamic book, the Koran. Nevertheless, he could not totally embrace either Christianity or Islam. Mohandas also continued to study Hinduism.

After resolving the claim's case for Abdullah, Gandhi was ready to return to India to rejoin his wife and children. However, at that time there was a bill before the Natal parliament to prevent Indians from voting. There emerged an outcry from Natal's Indians for Gandhi to stay and lead the fight against this bill. He said that he would not take fees for this public work, but there needed to be a guarantee for funds to pay for the costs of campaign - telegrams, printing, law books, travel, etc. There also needed to be adequate numbers of volunteers. Once this support was guaranteed, Gandhi agreed to stay in India and lead the campaign. Even though the bill passed despite a vigorous campaign, the process infused new life into the Indian community and Gandhi's ultimate life's dedication to justice began to emerge. The campaign brought together Indians of all faiths - Muslim, Hindu, Christian, Parsi, and a cross-section of socioeconomic classes. This led to a grassroots movement to have Gandhi stay in South Africa permanently. The 24 year old Gandhi said that he would still not take money for his public works, however, he queried whether he would have enough private legal work. In response 20 merchants gave Gandhi retainers to provide legal work for them. He then agreed to stay and rented a two story house on the beach in Durban. The application to be an advocate to the Natal Supreme Court was accepted. With that appointment he agreed to take off his turban when he was in the court. With Abdullah, Gandhi and others launched the Natal Indian Congress. Gandhi then began relating to the indentured Indian laborers. These laborers would take off their scarves when meeting a European or an important Indian.

Gandhi requested that these workers oppose this custom. He felt this was honoring some of the humiliation which they suffered.

Gandhi in South Africa, 1895

Gandhi's law practice was flourishing and thus his South African stay, particularly with the widespread Indian support, projected to last for some time. He therefore went back to India and brought his wife and children to South Africa. On his return to India Gandhi wrote a pamphlet, known as the Green Pamphlet because of the color that described the racist conditions of Indians in South Africa. Five thousand copies were printed. Soon every paper in India took note of the contents of the Green Pamphlet with summaries sent to London and Natal.

    Also in India he was impressed by the commitment to celibacy, which was called brahmacharya and even existed for a married man. This was a Hindu and Jain concept. Gandhi also became involved in sanitation efforts in response to the epidemic of plague in Bombay. Then, with Kasturba, his sons Harilal and Manilal, and a nephew Gokuldas they boarded the ship in Bombay for South Africa. A number of Durban whites were planning to prevent the Indians on ship, including Gandhi and his family, from landing because of the Green Pamphlet had publicly revealed South Afrikaners' treatment of Indians. Since there was no law to prevent such a landing, the plague in Bombay was used to institute a 23 day quarantine of passengers on the Gandhi ship. Finally when Gandhi left the ship he was pelted with stones and eggs as well as being kicked and slapped. He and his family finally reached their Beach Grove house and after a few days the climate improved. This was in part due to a published interview in which Gandhi refuted all of the charges that had been leveled at him. He also had shown courage and wisely did not press charges against his attackers. Also Natal's papers condemned the attackers.

Gandhi decided to have his children schooled by him. Unfortunately he did not have the time to provide adequate schooling for them and therefore his children suffered. An English governess was hired but proved inadequate to address the problem. In the meantime Kasturba delivered two more children, Ramdas and Devadas. At this time Gandhi was also moving toward a simpler life and he began washing and ironing his own clothes. In addition to his law practice, Gandhi also worked in a dispensary and obtained some medical skills. Some clerks from untouchable parents also lived in the Beach Grove home and Gandhi insisted on cleaning the chamber pots from their rooms. This led to a substantial conflict

Gandhi in the Boer War, 1988

with Kasturba.

In spite of Gandhi's nonviolence vow, he organized an ambulance corps of Indians for the British Empire during the Boer War. The war was ultimately won by the British against the Afrikaners (Boers). This was believed to forecast better rights for Indians, particularly in Natal. Thus Gandhi decided that it was time to return to India. Farewell gifts from the community were given to Gandhi, including gold chains, gold watches, diamond rings and there was also a gold necklace for Kasturba. Gandhi however refused the gifts and set up a trust for the community where all of the gifts, including Kasturba's necklace, were deposited.

Gandhi with the stretcher-bearers of the Indian Ambulance Corps during the Boer War, South-Africa.

On Gandhi's return to India he continued to articulate by various means the racial prejudice in South Africa against Indians. He first set up his law practice in Rajkot, but then was convinced to move to Bombay where he could better pursue his public work which ultimately was self-rule for India. His practice flourished in Bombay. Then he received a cable asking him to return to South Africa immediately. He believed that his stay would only be a few months, so he left Kasturba and the boys at their Santa Cruz home in Bombay. The issues were primarily in Transvaal, which was now under the British flag but run primarily by white Afrikaners of Dutch descent. The Indians who had left Transvaal during the Boer War were being required to apply to the Asian Department for permission to return to their homes. A delegation led by Gandhi brought their protest unsuccessfully to Joseph Chamberlain, Secretary of State for the colonies. Gandhi then decided to stay in Transvaal and to bring his family back to South Africa again from India. He set up his practice in Johannesburg and with the Transvaal Indians organized a Transvaal British Indian Association. His application to enroll in the Transvaal Supreme Court was surprisingly unopposed. The 33 year old Gandhi's target was the Asian Department which was requiring bribes from Indians requesting permission to return to their homes in Transvaal. In spite of compelling evidence the jury acquitted the person accused of requesting bribes, but the request for bribes to obtain entry permits stopped. This enhanced Gandhi's prestige.

Gandhi next focused on the ghetto where indentured Indians lived. The government was planning to abolish them without providing alternative dwellings. Gandhi appealed on behalf of the inhabitants and won all but one of his 70 cases. However, while the workers were awarded new quarters a plague epidemic occurred. With his medical experience Gandhi became actively involved in nursing the patients.

Gandhi supported the launching of a weekly journal in Durban called the Indian Opinion to be published in English, Gujarati; Tamil and Hindu. He agreed to write articles for the journal and if necessary to provide funding. Although Gandhi practiced restraint he did write about the inequalities of Indians in South Africa. Of interest, however, he rarely addressed the unfairness by which the blacks were treated. Realizing his commitments to the Indians in South Africa he again sent for Kasturba and his boys. They rented a two story house in a nice area of Johannesburg, but their home lives continued to become simpler. His family cleaned their own toilets and baked their own bread.

An uprising of the Zulus in Natal occurred because of unfair treatment by the whites. Gandhi offered the British Governor of Natal an Indian Ambulance Corp. The offer was accepted and Gandhi moved his family to Natal. On seeing the wounds of the unfortunate Zulus, Gandhi's Ambulance Corp cared for these blacks as well as the injuries to whites. The violence that he observed moved him even more towards a commitment to nonviolence and truth. He became committed to nonviolence resistance against injustice not only in South Africa but also India. He discussed chastity (brahmacharya) with Kasturba and committed completely to this vow as a component of purity.

Another fight emerged in Transvaal where a proposed new law required registration including finger and thumb prints by all Indians. Gandhi vehemently opposed this further humiliation of Indians and proposed a resolution of nonviolent resistance at all costs and penalties. In this regard Gandhi felt that Henry David Thoreau originated the idea of civil disobedience. Gandhi had coined the Indian term satyagraha which meant firmness for the truth. To oppose this anti-Indian legislature Gandhi sailed to London. In London for 6 weeks Gandhi met with many other public officials, spoke publically and wrote 5000 letters to plead for Indian rights in Transvaal. He met with 32 year old Winston Churchill who was Under Secretary for the Colonies. Churchill had been a reporter in the Boer war, was captured by the Afrikaners and then escaped. Churchill thought that as British subjects Indians in South Africa had rights, but refused to recommend interference with the Transvaal legislature's law. The British Registration Act (TARA), also called the Black Act by Indians, ultimately passed. In response a Passive Resistance Association was formed and hundreds of peaceful pickets were formed at the TARA offices. Gandhi wrote an Indian Opinion article encouraging passive resistance but spoke strongly against violence. He was calling the struggle satyagraha. Gandhi was arrested and sentenced to two months in the city jail. A compromise was proposed which stated that after voluntary registration by Indians the Black Act would be repealed. Gandhi agreed to the compromise but the Black Act was never repealed. Jan Smuts who was becoming the most powerful politician in South Africa, and who had forged the compromise, later said that because of strong white resistance he could not repeal the Black Act. In response thousands of Indians burned their registration certificates, and many were imprisoned including Gandhi for nine weeks in Pretoria. Some three to four thousand Indians were jailed in 1908 and 1909 including Gandhi's son, Harilal. The struggle for Indians in South Africa became even more difficult when nonviolent Indian protestors were being deported to India. Gandhi's national prestige in South Africa worked against him being deported. He made another trip to London to further appeal the registration law but was not optimistic. It was at a time when there was an effort to create the Union of South Africa from the Cape, Natal, Transvaal and Orange Free State colonies. The killing of Sir Curzon Wyllie by an Indian highlighted violence as a means of resistance. Gandhi, however, severely criticized the act and further emphasized the passive nonviolent resistance. On his trip back to South Africa Gandhi wrote his "Hind Swaraj" (Indian Self-Rule) which was strongly influenced by the writings of Leo Tolstoy and Thoreau. It was a 30,000 word manuscript. It was written to all Indians, not just Indians in South Africa. In essence he announced his life's mission to forge India self-rule by nonviolence. "Hind Swaraj" was published in the Indian Opinion in two issues in December 1909 and as a book in January 1910.

On return to South Africa a German Jew named Herman Kallenbach, who greatly admired Gandhi, gave him 1,100 acres some 21 miles from

Johannesburg. Shortly after Leo Tolstoy's death they decided to name the site Tolstoy Farm. Kallenbach and Gandhi had great love and respect for one another. The Tolstoy Farm had an abundance of oranges, apricots and plums, with a small house and a spring 500 yards from the house. Families of nonviolent disciples would learn and live there. Separate men's and women's residences were built along with a schoolhouse, a workshop for carpentry and shoemaking, as well as a house for Kallenbach. Hindus, Muslims and Christians all agreed to a totally vegetarian kitchen. Kallenbach learned to make sandals at a Trappist Monastery and taught Gandhi. The farm was to be totally self-supporting. The inhabitants sometimes walked 42 miles to Johannesburg and back. If they went by train, it was always third class. During Ramadan the Hindus fasted alongside with Muslims.

Gandhi hired a 17 year old to be his secretary, Sonja Schlesin, and she became a trusted colleague for major tasks as well as the finances. Henry Polak, 11 years younger than Kallenbach, became Gandhi's political representative and interpreter. Kallenbach was the financier and helper. Gandhi's struggles in the Union of South Africa continued. He supported a ban by India on the export of indentured Indian laborers to South Africa. He opposed a British three pound tax in Natal that every indentured laborer was being asked to pay. In 1912 Gokhale, President of the Indian National Congress, informed Gandhi that he was ready to visit South Africa. He saw Gandhi as his political successor in India and a major purpose of his visit to South Africa was to convince Gandhi to return to India. The visit was a great success and the Black Act was repealed and the racial ban for immigration to South Africa was removed.

Then the Cape Supreme Court declared that only marriages under Christian rites would be performed or registered by the Registration of Marriages in South Africa. Thus, Hindu, Muslim and Zoriastrian marriages were nullified. While the Indian businessmen were not eager to be involved in nonviolent protests with possible imprisonment, Gandhi found that the indentured workmen in the Natal coal mines, as well as women, including Kasturba, came forward to participate in passive resistance. Part of the protesters were moving across forbidden borders from Transvaal to Natal or from Natal to Transvaal. In one week there were 3000 strikes. Indian women from Transvaal were arrested and sentenced to three months of hard labor. Gandhi founded a new organization, Natal Indian Association, which started a striker's fund. When miners were ousted from their dwellings, Gandhi invited them to march 172 miles to the Tolstoy Farm in Transvaal where they could live and be fed. This became known as the Great March by the miners. Gandhi walked, ate and slept with them during the Great March. This sharing of hardship would become one of the reasons for Gandhi's remarkable leadership. The mine owners tried to negotiate with Gandhi, but he told them that the miners would only return to work once the 3 pound tax was repealed.

There were 2,037 men, 127 women and 57 children marching from Natal to Tolstoy Farm. One night during the march Gandhi was arrested, but he was able to obtain bail. There was a second arrest of Gandhi who again obtained bail. With his third arrest he told the 2000 marchers to continue without him in a peaceful, nonviolent manner. Gandhi was sent to Bloemfontein in the Orange Free State and was sentenced to 9 months in prison. Many of the marchers were taken back to Natal on trains and placed in the coal mines by the police. At this time they had marched for 110 miles. At one point in November 1913, the majority of Natal's 60,000 Indian workers were out on strike.

Gockhale from his sickbed in India publicized in India and Great Britain the action of Indian strikers in South Africa and their treatment. This led to a proposed settlement where Jan Smuts would form a three man commission to consider Gandhi's demands with an unwritten understanding that they would concede to his proposals. The commission requested that Gandhi,

Gandhi's ashram

Polak and Kallenbach be released from prison. Gandhi, dressed as an indentured worker, then addressed a nonviolent meeting in Durban. A settlement occurred in which the tax was abolished, Indian marriages were restored and the rights of former residents were assured. With the passage of this Indian Relief Bill the nonviolent protests were terminated.

With his nonviolent successes in South Africa in support of the poor Indian workers, Gandhi planned his departure from Cape Town to London in July 1914 en route to India. In many cities the martyrs of the struggles for freedom were honored as Gandhi bid farewell to South Africa. It was at this time that he became known as Mahatma, which meant great soul. Gandhi gave Smuts a pair of sandals that he personally had made. Later Smuts said that he did not feel worthy to wear Gandhi's shoes. He nevertheless wrote to a friend that he was glad that the saint had left South Africa's shores. Thus, to South Afrikaners, it was clear the Gandhi not only had great political instincts, but was courageous and unbending.

Gandhi was 45 years old when he returned to India, the land of his birth, which he had not seen for 12 years. Rudyard Kipling had written that three factors supported British rule and impeded Indian nationalism, namely the Muslim fear of Hindu rules, opposition of the native Princes and indifference of the majority of the agricultural population. The 1857 rebellion had been brutally suppressed by the British with the help of the Sikhs and Ghoorkas. On this background Gandhi's lifelong goal was for Indian self-rule (Hind Swaraj) through nonviolence (satyagraha) methods of civil disobedience. He felt that the poor, not the Indian elite, would be his primary partners in this struggle for freedom from the British Empire. He decided that in India he would only wear the clothing, not of the Europeans, but of the indentured poor workers of India. Gokhale, though unwell, traveled to Bombay to meet Gandhi's ship. He advised Gandhi, who was to be his successor in leading the Indian National Congress, initially to observe quietly as his student for a year. Of importance the Muslim barrister Muhammed Ali Jinnah was included in the receptions for Gandhi. At Gokhale's urging Gandhi met with the Bombay Governor Willington who requested that he be informed before Gandhi took any action against the Governor. Gandhi agreed to this request. Within four months Gandhi started in Amedabad an ashram, a religious retreat similar to Tolstoy Farm which he had established in South Africa. Those joining the ashram would pledge themselves to the following eleven vows: nonviolence, truth, non-stealing, chastity, non-possession, bread-labor, control of the palate, fearlessness, respect for all religions, Indian made things (swadeshi), and abolition of untouchability. Gandhi attacked the untouchability of the caste system for the remainder of his life. Unfortunately Gandhi's intended mentor, Gokhale, died within six weeks of Gandhi's return to India. With his freedom to speak now he gave a stirring speech to some militant students in which he detested assassination as a foreign growth. He said if the students were ready to die in the struggle for freedom he would die with them. This speech received great attention and among those affected were the Muslim Ali brothers, Muhammad (Oxford-trained) and Shaukat. They had protested against Britain's attitude toward Muslim Turkey which had sided with Germany in World War I. The Ali brothers bonded with Gandhi and supported his desire for Hindu-Muslim unity and respect for all religions. With the World War settlement the Turkish-led Ottoman Empire was disassembled and countries were created with British rule including Iraq, Jordan, Palestine, Egypt, as well as Syria under French rule. Thus the Muslim Khilafat of the Ottoman Empire was abolished.

When Gandhi admitted an untouchable couple to the ashram Kasturba and another couple protested. He told them that they could leave if they were unable to live with untouchables. Kasturba yielded and stayed, whereas the other couple left only to return later as Gandhi said, "having cleansed their hearts clean of untouchability." This is an example of Gandhi's passive resistance to social questions of inequality. Politically, he believed that self rule (Hind Swaraj) would not be obtained if opposed by untouchables or if Hindus and Muslims fought one another.

In December 1915 Gandhi attended his first Indian National Congress. The members heard a new voice - he identified with the poor, he approached the British as an equal, and he regarded every place in India as his home. Some saw him as a saint and others saw him as an impossible dreamer. Gandhi then traveled widely to Benares, Madras, Bombay, Karachi, and numerous small villages and large numbers came to hear him speak. Gandhi always traveled third class. He projected caring and strength. Gandhi said untouchability was a great crime against humanity. He pressed for unity between the Indian National Congress and the Muslim League and his weapon for Home Rule was always nonviolence. At a conference in Bombay Gandhi was joined by Jinnah and Sardar Vallabinbhai Patel, both of whom were London-trained lawyers. Before meeting Gandhi, Patel laughed about this strange man who thought that spinning yarn, grinding grain and cleaning lavatories would bring self rule for India. In meeting him, however, he recognized Gandhi as a serious and committed man.

In Lucknow Gandhi first met Jawaharlal Nehru who in the future Gandhi would call his heir. Nehru was a sophisticated 27 year old Kashmiri Brahmin who was also a lawyer. He had studied in London, Harrow and Cambridge, and was a moderate member of the Indian National Congress. In Parna, Bihar Gandhi was taken to the home of Rajendra Prasad who was unfortunately not there. His servants, however, thought Gandhi was a low caste and would not let him draw water from the well or use the lavatory in the house. Later, however, Prasad and Gandhi would become close colleagues and Prasad would be a future president of the Indian Congress. In north Bihar Gandhi found the peasants oppressed and forced by the British to grow indigo on part of their land even though the price was falling. Gandhi saw this as an opportunity to struggle for the peasants' rights using nonviolence. Prasad and other elite lawyers obtained statements from the peasants about the oppression of British rule. Gandhi then was asked by the government to leave the area on the next train but he refused. In court he indicated that he was following his conscience in supporting the peasants' complaints. These events were big news all around India and Gandhi was seen as a courageous man. The British Raj not only did not jail Gandhi, but allowed him to pursue the peasants' complaints as a member of an inquiry committee. The committee unanimously voted to remove the government's dictate on indigo growing. Another victory for Gandhi in 1917 was obtaining government agreement on a date to halt indentured emigration.

Gandhi with textile workers

Gandhi then enlisted Mahader Desai, a lawyer and gifted writer in both English and Gujarati, as a key aide. At age 25, Desai had translated Marley's "On Compromise" into Gujarati. Until his death in detention at age 50 years, Desai served Gandhi as a lawyer, stenographer, typist, confidante, interpreter, editor, helper, and friend. In 1918 in rural Gujarat torrential rains destroyed grain crops and Gandhi was asked to obtain a temporary suspension of the British land tax to help the destitute farmers. Gandhi convinced Patel to join him in the 5 month nonviolent campaign against the land tax. Over 3000 peasants signed a pledge to not pay the tax, even though some had their property seized when they refused to pay. The satyagraha (nonviolent campaign) led to the British Raj agreeing to forgo the tax for one year. With this victory Patel left his successful law practice and joined Gandhi in the ashram. Patel then lived with the workers, slept on the ground, washed his own clothes, and ate plain food. Thus Gandhi's associates lived with the common goal to struggle for freedom. Next Gandhi was asked to help Ahmedabad textile workers in their wage negotiations with the owners who had refused arbitration. In response Gandhi asked the workers to go on a nonviolent strike. Some workers returned to work when the owners offered a 20% raise; they had been asking for a 35% raise. With the strikers decreasing from 5000 to 1000 Gandhi changed his tactics. He declared a fast until the owners agreed to the 35% raise. Gandhi only stopped the fast when the owners agreed to a 35% increase in the workers very low wages.

With Great Britain involved in World War I with Germany, Turkey and the Austria-Hungarian countries, Gandhi had one of his most painful ethical dilemmas. Viceroy Chelmsford asked Gandhi to assist in recruiting Indians to fight on behalf of Britain in the war. In spite of his nonviolence principals, Gandhi believed that even after self rule a relationship with Great Britain would be important. There was not a good feeling in India about the British Raj, particularly after the fight over the land tax. Thus, despite Gandhi's effort, though they may have been half hearted, there was very little success in the recruitment efforts. Nevertheless, by the end of the war Gandhi was exhausted and affected with skin boils similar to what killed his father. Treatment at that time was to drink milk which was against Gandhi's vows. Kasturba, however, cleverly intervened and argued that his vow was only against cow's milk therefore he could drink goat's milk. Gandhi yielded to this logic, drank goat's milk and recovered.

This was also a time of turmoil in the Gandhi family. Kasturba and the four boys always felt that they were a secondary priority. They were angry that Gandhi never made education a priority for his sons. Manilal and Ramdas had returned to South Africa. Gandhi hoped that Manilal would take over "Indian Opinion" Journal which was in trouble and Ramdas decided to work with a tailor in Johannesburg. The oldest son, Harilal, had always wanted to study in London, but this was not supported by Gandhi. Harilal's wife died at a young age and he developed problems with alcoholism.

Gandhi's next challenge was against two British anti-sedition bills which authorized government arrests without trial and trials without appeal. There would be a two-year sentence for any Indian having any sedition material in his pocket. Desire for self rule was considered sedition by the British. Gandhi was outraged. He felt the bills showed the Raj's disrespect and contempt for Indians. Gandhi formed a committee of distinguished Indians who signed the following pledge:

> "We solemnly affirm that in the event of these Bills becoming law and until they are withdrawn we shall refuse civilly to obey these laws and such other laws as a Committee to be hereafter appointed may think fit, and we further affirm that we will be faithful to truth and refrain from violence to life, person and property."

This was the first time since 1857 where prominent Indians had publically defied British law. Since the Indian National Congress was not ready for nonviolent disobedience, Gandhi formed another group, Satyagrapha Sabha (nonviolent assembly), with him as president and Patel as secretary. He went to Delhi and told the Viceroy of his intentions. Next he was invited to Madras by a 40 year lawyer, Chakravarti Rajagopalachari, who was known as CR. When the Viceroy signed one of the bills, Gandhi called a protest involving suspended work, fasting, and prayer on the following Sunday. The Congress, however, did not support the call for a protest. What occurred was the first nation-wide political demonstration in India's history. Hindus and Muslims joined together to protest against the so-called Black Act Sedition Bill on Black Sunday. In Calcutta 200,000 Indians demonstrated. Villages, towns, the whole of India protested on the designated day. Unfortunately, not all of the protests were nonviolent and the Viceroy blamed Gandhi for the violence. Gandhi was asked to go to Punjab to help prevent violence. He was, however, removed from the train and sent back to Bombay before arriving in Punjab. The authorities claimed that his arrival in Punjab would cause violence. In contrast, Gandhi felt his presence would prevent violence. Violence leading to property destruction, cut telegraph wires, and deaths of both Europeans and Indians occurred. Gandhi was very disappointed and Patel read the weakened Gandhi speech in Gujarat to over 10,000 people.

Gandhi stated that he would repent and do penance for his responsibility in exciting violence.

The Amritsar massacre was the worst of the British rule. On April 13, 1919 General Dyer banned public meetings but not everyone knew about the ban. Over 10,000 unarmed Hindus, Muslims and Sikhs gathered for a meeting at an open ground (Jallianwalla Bagh) which was enclosed by five foot walls on three sides. Dyer and 50 soldiers with rifles entered on the fourth side which was the only exit and opened fire without warning. The shooting lasted 10 minutes and 379 were killed and 1000 injured. Dyer then demanded that every Indian crawl in the street because a British woman (Miss Sherwood) had been attacked. He also demanded that Indians salute every British officer they saw. Violators of these regulations were flogged at a public whipping post. Gandhi called the Viceroy in strong protest of these actions by the British.

Gandhi was asked to take over editorship of "Young Indian" which would become a weekly and be published in Amedabad as well as the weekly "Navajivan." Gandhi then possessed the communication vehicles to send his struggle for freedom message throughout India. One of his messages was that the destruction of Indian weaving by the British had been a factor in the country's poverty. He therefore encouraged Indians to take up the spinning wheel (charkha) to provide yarn and handlooms for weaving cloth. This further led to hand-spun and hand-woven clothes (khadi) becoming popular throughout India. This led to a relative boycott in India on British textiles. Every man and woman who wore or wove khadi felt tied to Mahatma Gandhi, to the poor, to self-rule, and to nonviolence.

The 50 year old Gandhi demanded from the British Raj an investigation of the Armritsar massacre and for punishments to follow. This was undertaken by the Hunter Commission, but Gandhi also entered Punjab and organized a parallel investigation. The annual Congress met in Armritsar and the Ali brothers, who had been released, attended. Gandhi drafted a resolution condemning the massacre and also the violence by the Indian mobs. In response the British Commissioner of Ahmedabad, Frederick Pratt, congratulated Gandhi and reached out a hand of "fellowship and cooperation." However, the Hunter report absolved the Punjab governor of responsibility for the Armritsar massacre and General Dyer was only criticized for "bad judgment." Moreover, the House of Lords passed a motion in support of Dyer and he received a sword of honor and 20,000 British pounds from admirers.

In May the Treaty of Serres gave Sunni and Shia Islam's holiest sites to British mandates. For example, Mecca and Medina were placed under a pro-British chieftain. Iraq with Karbala and Palestine with Jerusalem also became British mandates. Thus, along with the Armritsar massacre, Hindus and Muslims were united in their anti-British resentment. Gandhi then outlined his non-cooperation with the British in a Young Indian article. They included return of titles and honorary posts, quitting civilian posts in government, withdrawal from police and military, and not paying taxes. He emphasized that all non-cooperation must be nonviolent. At that time Gandhi accepted the Presidency of the All-Indian Home Rule League, an important platform for his non-cooperation, nonviolent plans against the British rule. He announced the beginning of non-cooperation even before the All-Indian Congress meeting. His campaign would begin unless the British terms for dismantling the Turkish Ottoman Empire (Khilafat movement) were revised and the Armristar massacre in Punjab was redressed. Neither of Gandhi's demands were met by the British Raj. So in 1920 at age 50 Gandhi took on the powerful British empire. He explained to the British Viceroy that it was his non-cooperative approach that prevented violence. Gandhi returned the British medals which he had received for his freedom struggles in South Africa. His non-cooperation campaign began to spread across India. A free Indian flag was proposed in three colors - orange for Hindus, green for Muslims, and white to represent all others such as Sikhs, Christians, Parsi, and Jews. The flag would be made of khadi and the spinning wheel would be featured on the flag. Gandhi wrote and spoke frequently and strongly about cruelties against untouchables.

There were hurdles to Gandhi's non-cooperation campaign for Indian self rule. The renowned poet, Tagore, urged Gandhi to unite not divide East and West of the world.

Gandhi and renowned poet Rabindranath Tagore in 1940

Gandhi replied that his movement would lead to honorable and mutually respected unity rather than subordinate unity under the West's dominance. He also said that the millions of hungry Indians deserved primarily one poem - food. The non-cooperation campaign led to shrinking of the Empire's authority. Revenues from alcohol sales decreased, disagreements were settled out of British courts, and foreign textiles including hats, caps, suits and shawls were burned. The number of women wearing burqas decreased. As Gandhi traveled around India throngs of Indians waited at all hours to see him. The pressures led him to declare that perfect truth is silence. He therefore decided not to speak on Mondays and practiced this silent Monday the rest of his life. To compete with the foreign mode, ankle length loin cloths, he began wearing a waist to knee garment (dhoti).

When riots broke out in Bombay the British Raj declared a ban on meetings and censored the press. Gandhi's response was to continue non-cooperation even if it meant imprisonment. This lead to about 30,000 Indians being imprisoned. With the Prince of Wales' planned visit to India approaching, Viceroy Reading sought negotiations with Gandhi. Gandhi demanded the release of political prisoners, the lifting of bans and full freedom of all Congress workers. Unfortunately a set back to the nonviolence campaign occurred. About 4000 Hindus and Muslims surrounded a police station in the small town of Chauri Chaura and two of them were killed by the police. This led to burning of the police station and 22 police were killed by the crowd while yelling, "Victory to Mahatma Gandhi." This led to Gandhi calling off a planned protest in Bardoli for which he was criticized. His alternative constructive program which was approved by the Congress Working Group included:

- Recruit Congress workers who were committed to truth and nonviolence
- Spin yarn daily in every home for prosperity and freedom
- Visit untouchable homes damaged by alcohol
- Establish village councils

Next Gandhi was arrested and sentenced to six years imprisonment. He had pleaded guilty for his responsibility for the Chauri Chaura violence. In prison Gandhi had uninterrupted time to read. He consumed many writings including Gibbon's "Rise and Fall of the Roman Empire," Plato, Walter Scott, Goethe's Faust, Tagore, and many others. He read several Christian, Muslim and Buddhist books. Two years after his arrest his poor health led to the government releasing him. Ultimately the emaciated Gandhi was found to have appendicitis at surgery. On discharge he decided not to lead another attack on the Raj until March 1928 when his six year sentence would have expired. He also began thinking about his successor as India's leader in the freedom struggle. Also there had emerged resistance to his non-cooperation, nonviolence movement. The Hindu-Muslim tension reemerged and involved violence inflamed by a poem denigrating the Prophet Mohammed. Gandhi's response was to declare a 21 day fast except for water as penance. He started his fast in Mohammed Ali's home in Delhi. All across India everyone was concerned about the fast and Gandhi's health. The Ali brothers responded positively for Hindu-Muslim unity and Gandhi ended his fast. After 1924 Gandhi enhanced his campaign against untouchability, dowry, and liquor and in support of khadi clothes and nonviolence.

Madeline Slade, a 33 year old daughter of a British admiral, decided to join Gandhi, having been inspired by Tolstoy's writings about pacifism. She joined Gandhi's ashram and took the name Mira. She learned to spin, speak Hindustan and clean lavatories. She became Gandhi's helper, ally and disciple. Gandhi continued to travel and speak widely throughout India. Shortly thereafter in April 1928 his close ashram associate, Maganal, died. Maganal's skills were in carpentry, weaving, printing, engineering and managing. Gandhi was heartbroken. As Gandhi neared his 60th birthday, he continued to travel but seemed more aware of his mortality. In this regard he began thinking about his political successor. Since his 1924 fast Gandhi had turned his eyes on Jawaharlal Nehru, a London trained barrister who was strongly against British oppression. He was 20 years younger than Gandhi, but his fascination with Marxism bothered Gandhi.

In October 1927 the new Viceroy for India called Gandhi to Delhi and informed him that Sir John Simon would tour India, then he would make proposals about a constitution for India. This Simon Commission was all white and included no Indians, suggesting that only British could contribute to an Indian constitution. The Congress with Gandhi's support voted to boycott the Commission. The slogan "Simon Go Back" became the cry everywhere the Commission traveled. In 1928, Gandhi's deadline to reinstate the nonviolence struggle for freedom, the British land tax was increased by 22% in Bardoli. The peasants wanted to defy this tax and asked for Gandhi's and Patel's help. In a nonviolent protest the peasants refused to pay the tax and the British confiscated their land and cattle. After four months the British yielded and the tax was discontinued with most of the property returned.

At the Indian National Congress in Calcutta, Nehru supported Complete Independence. However, Gandhi's December 31, 1929 deadline for Dominion status (like Canada and Australia) or Complete Independence would prevail. Jinnah and Mohammed Ali brought to Delhi constitution proposals for Muslim majorities in Bengal and Punjab legislatures and a one-third representation for Muslims on the Central Assembly. When the Congress did not support these Muslim proposals Jinnah, president of the Muslim League, talked about leaving the Congress and Mohammed Ali actually did. Gandhi was offered the presidency of the Congress, but citing his own lack of energy he recommended Nehru. Gandhi cited Nehru's youth, determination, integrity and courage while admitting that they had their political differences. Nehru thus became president of the Congress. Viceroy Irwin proposed talks in London with Indian leaders. Gandhi asked whether these discussions would start with Dominion status. When Irvin did not agree, the Congress pledged to strive for Complete Independence. Gandhi was then asked by his supporters how the campaign for independence should commence. He suggested raising the tricolor flag throughout India and having Congress members resign from the legislatures. Gandhi would designate the time for the campaign to begin, but he had not decided about the nature of the independence campaign except that it must be nonviolent. The first stage would involve only individuals from ashrams which were trained and committed to nonviolence. Also, if violence entered the movement he would halt the campaign.

Finally, Gandhi arrived at his strategy for the campaign. By taxing the sale and manufacture of salt, the British government was hurting the poor and sick Indians. Gandhi projected a walk to the beach where the salt was. They would then gather and sell the "illegal" salt that they had collected. All Indians, Hindus and Muslims, peasants and untouchables, could support defiance against

The Salt March

the Salt Tax. Moreover, in contrast to the land tax, the British could not justify taking away land or cattle in reprisal to the Indian opposition to the Salt Tax. The Salt march was to be about 200 miles to the coast where waves from the Arabian Sea had left layers of salt. The initial march would include about 80 physically and morally strong members of the ashram. The 61 year old Gandhi expected to get arrested, jailed and might even die as a part of the Salt Tax campaign. All marchers wore khadi clothes and were fed simple food by the villagers along the way. In one village he walked directly to the untouchables quarters, to the dismay of the high cost greeters, and drew drinking water from the untouchables' well. To Gandhi's surprise after 24 days the marchers arrived at the coast without interference from the British. The Salt Tax march had received worldwide attention. Many journalists from India and elsewhere were awaiting the marchers on their arrival at the coast. Gandhi's message to them was "I want world support in this battle of Right against Might." Gandhi scooped up salt with his hands and subsequently hundreds of thousands of Indians emulated this "illegal" act. Nehru said that it was like releasing a spring. The Raj's response was to ban Indian newspapers and the Congress Working Committee. Many protesters were beaten rather than arrested since the jails were full. More and more Indian women and girls were becoming involved in the Salt Tax campaign. Gandhi was supportive and suggested that women may have more moral power, be more self-sacrificing, and have greater powers of courage and endurance than men. Women picketed the sale of liquor and foreign clothes.

Gandhi decided to lead a raid on the British government salt depots and he told Viceroy Irwin about his plan. The police then entered his camp at midnight and arrested Gandhi. The marchers still set out towards the salt depot and were surrounded, beaten, and some arrested by several hundred police. About 90,000 Indians were arrested including Nehru and Patel. Earlier Nehru had doubts about the nonviolent campaign, but later he wrote Gandhi about the new India Gandhi had created with his campaign.

Gandhi did not know how long he would be imprisoned. He wrote about 60-80 letters every week, many to members of his ashram. He wrote to Kasturba, Mira, his children Devadas and Manilal, and many others. The British initiated negotiations with Gandhi, Nehru, and others who asked the British to concede the right of India to leave the Empire as well as free collection of salt. These demands were rejected by the British. There was a pact, however, with Viceroy Irwin and Gandhi in which tens of thousands of Indians were released from prison. With the pact, men and women could freely collect salt and picket cloth and liquor shops. The pact implied equality between Britain and India, Viceroy and Gandhi, Raj and the Congress, and between Raj policemen and nonviolent law breakers. However, a new Viceroy was appointed, Lord Willingdon, and many violations of the pact occurred and were ignored by the new Viceroy. Gandhi then was invited to London for a Round Table Discussion (RTD). While in London Churchill would not meet with Gandhi and objected to Gandhi's loin cloth attire. Gandhi's first speech to the RTD was described by the young reporter, William Shirer, as the greatest of Gandhi's long political career. Shirer would later become quite famous with this book "The Rise and Fall of the Third Reich." Gandhi also traveled and spoke widely around Britain in an effort to explain India's freedom struggle to the British people. At the reception for the Indian delegates with King George, Gandhi was asked if he felt uncomfortable wearing his loin cloth. Gandhi replied that he was comfortable in his dress and that the King had enough clothes on for both of them. Gandhi met Bernard Shaw, Charlie Chaplin, former Prime Minister Lloyd George, his old friend/foe Jan Smuts, and many others. He pleaded unsuccessfully with the British Minister for a time table for Indian Independence. The British pointed out that the Congress did not have the right to be the voice for India. One example was 40 year old Bhimrad Ambedkar, born an untouchable, who became a brilliant scholar with doctorates from London and New York. He believed that he represented the untouchables, not Gandhi. Ambedkar wanted a separate electorate for the untouchables which Gandhi rejected. On leaving London the British made it clear to Gandhi that they would crush any rebellion for independence. After his 3 month stay, Gandhi said that he came seeking peace and returned to India fearing war. On arrival in Bombay Kasturba told Gandhi that Nehru had been arrested. On January 4, 1931 Gandhi and Patel were arrested and the Indian National Congress was banned. Viceroy Willingdon imposed press censorship, defying peasants lost more land, and offices and ashrams related to the Congress were raided. In January and February 75,000 Indians were arrested and 300-400 thousand Indians were beaten with lathis (sticks or staffs). Gandhi decided that if the British transferred power to the provinces with the Constitution, Indians should capture the legislatures. The provinces could then restore the lost land to the peasants. With the British proposal that untouchables would be given a separate electorate, Gandhi committed to fast in protest. A day before the fast was to begin Hindu leaders resolved that with self rule the parliament would assure that untouchables would have equal access to public wells, public schools, public roads, and all other public institutions. Nevertheless Gandhi started his fast. Tagore was very concerned and visited Gandhi on his cot under a mango tree in the prison courtyard. In response to Gandhi's fast the untouchables and the caste Hindus signed an agreement which was cabled to London where the British minister accepted it. The agreement stated that there would be a common electorate but with a guaranteed number of seats for the untouchables. With this agreement (Poona Pact) Gandhi halted his fast.

In spite of the Pact, the British felt they had made substantial gains. Gandhi was still behind bars and his journals were banned. With his success on the untouchable issues, Gandhi began calling the untouchables Harijans (People of God). He continued to emphasize that the untouchables had been treated like lepers, economically worse than slaves, not allowed to enter houses of God or use public schools, hospitals, or parks. Caste Hindu doctors or lawyers will not serve them. Gandhi started another journal named Harijan.

When Gandhi was not allowed to work on Harijan journal in his prison cell, he began a fast on August 16, 1933 at age 64. On August 20 his condition worsened and he was moved to the hospital. He was unconditionally released 3 days later when it looked like he would not survive. At this time Gandhi wondered if British repression had defeated his nonviolence approach. When British gave wide powers to the provinces, Gandhi's strategy was to enter Raj's councils and capture power in the provinces. In November with increased strength Gandhi again began traveling throughout India where he drew immense crowds. Nehru, who was still in prison, was worried that Gandhi's focus on untouchables would dilute India's struggle for self rule. Gandhi however felt that India's independence necessitated the support of the untouchables. Kasturba was then released from jail in June and was able to join Gandhi. Because of his support for untouchables there were caste Hindus who were violently against Gandhi. There were arrests of those considering attacking Gandhi, one with an ax and another with a lathi. There was also a bomb thrown at a car thought to be carrying Gandhi. He in fact was in another car. Nehru was released from jail because of his wife's illness. He was disappointed by Gandhi's cessation of the disobedience campaign. There had developed a polarization in the Indian Congress with Nehru on the left and others on the right. Gandhi felt reconciliation could be achieved better without him so he resigned from the Congress.

The British Parliament passed the Act of 1935 which gave substantial autonomy to the provincial legislatures, but maintained British control over the Central Assembly.

Nehru and Gandhi

With Nehru's release Gandhi asked him to succeed Prasad in 1935 as president of the Congress and he agreed. Nehru believed in socialism and argued with Patel who was skeptical about socialism. At the Lucknow Congress the appointed Working Committee was divided between socialists and Gandhi's old guard of Patel, Prasad, and CR. Nehru became president but within weeks there was conflict when Nehru said that he had consented to the Working Committee's opinion in spite of his better judgment. This led to seven members of the Working Committee resigning. Gandhi, however, intervened and the resignations were rescinded.

Gandhi decided to move to a small village among untouchables with Kasturba. They lived in a small mud hut as did Mira. The village was renamed Sevagram (village of service). It grew and became Gandhi's next ashram where aides and allies joined him. There, in his late sixties, Gandhi developed malaria, nevertheless he introduced weaving, spinning and tanning to the villagers. From 1937-39 Gandhi's political focus related to Congress members capturing provincial offices. He felt that the British were sincere about allowing freedoms at the provincial level and recommended Congress accepting these offices.

Jinnah and Gandhi

In July 1937 eight Congressmen were installed as premiers in provinces. Jinnah then started to unite the Muslim League against the Indian National Congress even as Congress grew in power and popularity throughout India. There was momentum occurring towards self government. Yet, as independence appeared near, the separation between Hindus and Muslims seemed to grow. Jinnah asked Gandhi to meet him at his home in Bombay on the basis that the League represents Muslim India and the Congress represents Hindu India. This was a major blow to Gandhi's dream of Hindu-Muslim unity as the basis of a self-governing Indian nation. Gandhi found Jinnah immoveable in his position and their talks were unsuccessful. With other Muslim leaders, however, he had more

Gandhi spinning, 1929

success in convincing them the need for Hindu-Muslim unity.

At the same time in Europe Neville Chamberlin made an agreement with Hitler that allowed the Nazi takeover of Czechoslovakia. Gandhi said that this was a peace at the cost of honor. He also said that if there was ever a humane reason for war, Hitler's persecution of the entire Jewish race was such a reason. He nevertheless said he was against war. With Congress president Subhas Bose admiring Mussolini, Gandhi was anxious for him not to be reelected. Prasad was elected Congress president. With war between Britain and Germany being likely, and the anti-British feeling in India, the time seemed right for the defiance campaign to reemerge against the Raj. Of interest, at that time African-Americans were seeking Gandhi's advice about their struggle for freedom. He told them that with right on their side and with nonviolence as their only weapon, a bright future for them was assured.

A source of criticism of Gandhi was his remedy for his tendency to shiver. He would find relief through women sleeping with him. With Kasturba's full knowledge he called these women his daughters or sisters. Gandhi also felt that this tested the strength of his character and vow of celibacy. Sushila Nayyar, a 24 year old doctor, was one of his aides who frequently slept with him. Mira asked Gandhi to stop sleeping with women and he agreed temporarily even though Sushila protested. His routine in Sevagram was to awake at 3:30 am (he slept 4 hours a day), praying twice a day, spinning yarn for an hour and spending time with the sick. He walked several miles a day and ate carefully.

When Hitler's army moved into Poland, Britain declared war on Germany on September 1, 1939. In May 1939 the All-India Congress Committee had opposed all attempts by the British to impose a war involving India without approval of the Indian people. Yet with Britain's declaration of war Viceroy Linlithgow announced that India too was at war. Gandhi knew that Indians would not support the war without a commitment for Complete Independence at the end of the war. In contrast the British Parliament empowered the Viceroy to override or take over the provincial governments. Gandhi's proposal of unconditional nonviolent support for Britain in the war was rejected unanimously by the Congress Working Committee. The Viceroy further stated that the Congress request for political independence at the end of the war would not be granted.

Jinnah, representing the Muslim League, did not ask for independence from the British but rather asked that any Constitution would protect Muslim rights. To Jinnah, it appeared like the Hindus, not Britain, were the enemy. The Raj would only say to Congress that after the war they could hold constitutional talks with the British government. In response the Congress Working Committee asked all provincial ministers to resign. With Jinnah's support there was a movement by the Muslim League at their Lahore Meeting to have separate Muslim states where Muslims would be in the majority. This became known as the Pakistan resolution. In response to this Muslim movement, a Muslim, Abdul Azad was named president of the Congress. Azad, along with Gandhi, supported Hindu-Muslim unity in India. Jinnah however responded that he would give his life to achieve a Muslim state. He was adamant in his belief that the Congress was a Hindu, not an

Gandhi and Patel

Indian Body. Gandhi believed the British approach was to divide Hindus and Muslims, so the Raj would continue to rule. When Churchill became Britain's Prime Minister shortly after the fall of France, it was clear to Gandhi that independence for India would be even more difficult because of Churchill's attachment to the British Empire. Moreover, the Congress Working Committee including President Azad and Patel rejected Gandhi's nonviolence commitment in the fight against Hitler. Tens of thousands of Indian recruits were joining the British war. However, Gandhi organized a campaign of individual civil disobedience. The slogan was to be, "It is wrong to help the British war with men or money. The only worthy effort is to resist all war with nonviolent resistance." The candidates chosen to state this slogan, and thus be arrested, had to support nonviolence, spinning, caste equality, and Hindu-Muslim friendship. Nehru, Patel, Prasad, CR and hundreds of others were jailed. Initially Gandhi did not participate for fear of precipitating a nationwide mass disobedience campaign which would lead to British repressive brutality. On December 4, 1941, however, the British released all the civil disobedience protestors.

After the fall of Singapore, Malaya, and Rangoon to the Japanese,

Churchill sent a proposal from the War Cabinet to Indians. It included full Dominion status with the right of secession from the Commonwealth for Indians after the war; a post-war Constitutional Assembly with elected members by provincial legislature and an immediate national government composed of representatives of the leading political parties. Gandhi did not like an implied balkanization of India (e.g. separate Hindu and Muslim states), nomination of princes and that India's defense would be controlled totally by Britain. Gandhi's response was the "Quit India" campaign asking the British to leave India and pledging a nonviolent, non-cooperation against the Japanese if they invaded India. Nehru's similar but alternative resolution was approved by the Working Committee stating that the British should not retain any control or authority in India, but allied troops, if needed, could prevent Japanese occupation. The Congress passed the Quit India resolution and discussions began about an action plan. The ideas included nonviolence, students should leave government colleges, stoppage of work, withhold the land and salt tax, government servants should resign, and there should be no interruption of the defense of China and Russia. Gandhi did not feel that he would be arrested until he broke the law. Nevertheless, on August 9, before the Quit India action plan was launched, Gandhi was arrested. It was generally believed that the 73 year old Gandhi would not survive the imprisonment. The Working Committee was arrested and when Kasturba was going to speak she and Sushila were arrested. The Congress was banned, the press was further censored and public meetings were prohibited. With these events by the British India erupted into nation-wide protests. In response the Raj police killed over 1,000 protesting Indians. Per Gandhi's suggestion, the protestors everywhere were shouting "Do or Die." The British arrested over 100,000 protestors, and beat even more. The uprising was quelled by the British violence. Unfortunately despite Gandhi's pleas the eruption was not nonviolent by the protestors. Bridges were destroyed, telegraph and telephone wires were cut, police and post offices were burned, and some Raj employees were killed. Some nonviolent believers felt that it was wrong to attack people but alright to destroy property. Gandhi disagreed. The Quit India campaign had negative consequences, and it destroyed irrevocably any chance of any reconciliation between the British and Indians. To Gandhi's great sorrow, Mahader Desai, his close colleague, died suddenly age 50 during the eruption. After the violence Gandhi commenced a 21 day fast, the technique which he had used on several occasions to give him voice with the Indian population. One consequence of Gandhi's Quit India campaign was that Nehru, Patel, Azad, and others decided that in the future there would be more hesitation in following Gandhi's instincts. It had brought the imprisonment and suffering of many, and strength to the Muslim League. During Kasturba's imprisonment her health continued to decline. At the same time there was famine and starvation in Bengal which led Gandhi to request unsuccessfully the release of the Congress Working Group to allow them to address the Bengali tragedy. The new Viceroy Wavell, like the old Viceroy, asked Gandhi to withdraw the Quit India resolution as a priority of negotiation.

During Gandhi's 21 day fast Kasturba was supportive and ever present. She was however embittered by her prison confinement and at 74 years of age she died in Gandhi's arms having suffered several heart attacks. Gandhi said that Kasturba and he had become one and she was the better half. They had been married for 62 years. While Gandhi always seemed unbowed and optimistic, the losses of Kasturba and Muhader Desai led to evidence of depression at a time when he was also suffering from malaria and dysentery. The prison physicians evaluated Gandhi's deteriorating condition and the Viceroy felt that he would be unable to participate in politics in his weakened condition. Moreover, the negative feeling against the government would be accentuated if Gandhi died in prison; therefore in May 1944 he released Gandhi and his entourage. Churchill hated Viceroy Wavell's decision to release Gandhi, particularly after Gandhi appeared to regain his strength.

In discussions with the Viceroy Gandhi expressed his belief that freedom in India from British rule would impact the hope for freedom elsewhere in Asia and Africa and even for Negroes in America. Churchill was against any negotiations between the Viceroy and the "half-naked fakir," i.e. Gandhi. Gandhi however traveled to Bombay to meet Jinnah who over 29 years earlier had welcomed him to India from South Africa. There was no question that Jinnah was the leader of the Muslim League with its two million members and the strongest supporter of the Pakistan resolution. Although ill with pneumonia, which probably was tuberculosis, Jinnah had a sharp mind and a steel will. Jinnah and Gandhi met some fourteen times at Jinnah's home. Their talks received great attention from the press but failed. Jinnah wanted the British to divide India before independence because he felt that post-independence a separate Pakistan state would be more difficult to obtain. The Bombay talks increased Jinnah's popularity with Muslims who saw him as the secular savior of Islam. On Gandhi's return to Sevagram there were 3,000 letters waiting for his reply and his non-political interests had been ignored including the village industries, a common language for India, basic education for all Indians, and forming a Kasturba Trust. At the same time while Gandhi was recuperating in Sevagram, Viceroy Wavell was lobbying Churchill to allow him to release the Congress Working Group. After eight months of lobbying and a trip to London Wavell was successful. The war in Europe ended in May 1945 and Wavell announced the Working Group release on June 14, 1945. In July 1945, the Labor party won the British election and Clement Atlee replaced Churchill as Prime Minister. Atlee agreed with Wavell that elections in India should be held for the Central Assembly and the provincial legislatures. Gandhi, who was 76 years old, initiated discussions with Nehru, his designated heir. As noted, Nehru had socialist leanings and did not believe that the villages should embody nonviolence and truth. He felt that villages were backward culturally and intellectually whereas Gandhi believed the focus needed to be on improving life in the villages. The election results for the General Assembly were quite polarized - the Congress won virtually all of the non-Muslim seats and the Muslim League won virtually all of the Muslim seats. In January 1946 Atlee told the House of Commons that Britain would quit India and three ministers were sent to India to negotiate the country's independence. Viceroy Wavell invited Gandhi to the talks in Delhi, but the Working Committee would represent the Congress. Azad had been president of the Congress for six years, but much of the time he was in prison. He desired reelection but Gandhi favored Nehru. The Congress president was likely to become Prime Minister of an Independent India. The British ministers had two goals for the talks in Delhi - resolve the Pakistan question and convert the Viceroy's Executive Council into an interim national government. The ministers favored neither a small Pakistan with Punjab and Bengal divided nor a large Pakistan with all of Punjab and Bengal. In the end Jinnah accepted the smaller area in exchange for sovereignty for Pakistan. The negotiations about the interim government were also very contentious. Gandh desired Hindu-Muslim unity while Jinnah desired for the Congress only to represent Hindus and the Muslim League to only represent the Muslims. Gandhi's hope for Indian unity with Congress representing all religions in

India was supported by Azad, a Muslim, who was president of the Congress. At the next Congress meeting Nehru replaced Azad as the Congress president. In Bombay the Congress accepted, against Gandhi's advice, a Constitutional Assembly which allowed the Muslim League the future possibility to secede and become an independent Pakistan. Jinnah was however not satisfied and he declared "direct action" to achieve an independent Pakistan. This led in Calcutta to youths shouting Pakistan and killings of Hindus by Muslims, then retaliatory killings of Muslims by Hindus occurred. Gandhi, who was now 77 years old, proceeded to travel to Calcutta and East Bengal to prevent further violence. At one of his prayer meetings 15,000 attended, 80 percent of whom were Muslims. Jinnah made a statement that vengeance and retaliation were not part of Islam and in an independent Pakistan all minorities would have security of life and property just like Muslims. To address the violence around him Gandhi believed that he needed to enforce his chastity test. He therefore began sleeping with Manu, his 19 year old grandniece, against the advice of several friends and colleagues. Manu would also cook for him and assist him in his chores. Sushila was quite upset with Gandhi's chastity test with Manu. Gandhi however felt that a successful chastity test (yagra) with Manu would give him the strength to quell the Bengal violence. Even though a third party was always present and their sleep was undisturbed, Gandhi and Manu agreed to suspend the yagra on the advice of many.

Gandhi began visiting villages on foot, carrying a long bamboo stick, but not walking more than four miles in one day. A mobile hut was brought with him. Hindus and Muslims greeted him during his trek where he visited 47 different villages over two months. At the various villages he was hosted by cobblers, weavers, fishermen, and farmers, and preached nonviolence, love, Hindu-Muslim unity, and acceptance of untouchables. He walked bare footed and proclaimed that he could not wear shoes on holy ground where people had lost loved ones to violence. About 100 villagers carrying the Congress flag and a dozen journalists accompanied him on his journey through villages. The impact of his village visits was to give Hindus confidence and Muslims a change of heart. In some places Muslims declared that they would risk their lives protecting Hindus. When asked about religious instruction in schools, the very religious Gandhi said that religion is a personal matter and schools should teach ethics not religion. During his trip to villages, he slept only four hours a day with the remainder of his time listening and speaking to villagers, spinning, writing, treating the sick, and of course walking.

Gandhi had some dark thoughts that India was moving towards partition and more violence, a premonition which became true. Prime Minister Atlee announced on February 20, 1947 that Britain would leave India by June 1948 which was some 16 months away. Neither Nehru, Patel, CR, Azad, and Prasad nor the Congress President Kripalani consulted with Gandhi after the London announcement. Violence began in Punjab when Hindu and Sikh leaders announced an Anti-Pakistan Day. At least 1000 people were killed, mostly Hindus and Sikhs. Ultimately there became a partition of two Punjabs and two Bengals. In Behar, Bengal 7,000 Muslims had been killed and nearly 10,000 homes destroyed. More than 100,000 Muslims migrated to Bengal. The Muslim League called the killings genocide by the "Hindu Congress." At the same time Punjab was also ready to have out of control violence and killing. Gandhi had suggested Jinnah for Prime Minister, believing that he would control violence, but his proposal was rejected. Jinnah and Gandhi signed a joint appeal denouncing all forms of violence throughout the country. On April 20, 1947 Nehru publically declared support for the Pakistan partition.

On June 3, 1947 the partition plan was negotiated with the Congress, Muslim League and the British government. Gandhi thought that the partition would lead to more violence but the Working Committee felt that partition would lead to more peace. Many Hindus criticized Gandhi for not fasting to death in protest to partition. Of interest Gandhi forewarned that an arms race might occur between India and Pakistan. This happened with both India and Pakistan becoming nuclear powers. On August 15, 1947, the day of Independence, Gandhi was in a Muslim home in one of the poorest areas of Calcutta. The city was peaceful and on August 18, 1947 a half million Hindus and Muslims attended Gandhi's prayer meeting. He advised the new ministers to be humble, beware of pageantry and power which can corrupt and remember they are to serve the poor in the villages.

Gandhi having tea with Mountbatten, 1947

On Independence Day things were different in Punjab. Gandhi offered to go to Punjab but Nehru and Patel felt it could be too dangerous for him. Governor-General Mountbatten wrote to Gandhi, "In Punjab we have 55,000 troops and large sects rioting whereas in Bengal our forces are one man (i.e. Gandhi) and there is no rioting." However, some violence did break out in Calcutta and Gandhi decided to fast until peace returned. The fast started on September 1 and had an immediate effect to decrease violence. In sympathy with Gandhi 500 Calcutta police went on a 24 hour fast. On September 4 a delegation came, including Muslims and Sikhs, and pledged to risk their lives to prevent any occurrence of violence if Gandhi would stop his fast. Gandhi agreed. With peace restored in Calcutta, Gandhi sent Nehru a telegram that he was coming to Punjab. No one was spared the violence and savagery in Punjab, not even women with children or the aged. Each side was merciless. By the end of September over 250,000 Muslims and non-Muslims had died. Moreover, women were being raped and abducted. The two way flow of Hindus and Sikhs eastward and Muslims westward would continue until the summer of 1948. This Great Migration involved 5.5 million Hindus and Sikhs moving to India and an equal number of Muslims moving to Pakistan. En route to Punjab Gandhi stopped in Delhi where Premier Nehru and Deputy Premier Patel met him and he saw the violence in that city. A taxi driver said that had Gandhi arrived a few days later there would not have been a Muslim alive in Delhi. The Muslims in Pakistan and the Hindus and Sikhs in India undertook equivalent barbarism in the sake of revenge. Churchill's comments implied an "I told you so" attitude.

On his 77th birthday, Gandhi was greeted by Nehru, Patel, Lady Mountbatten and others. When visitors called him Mahatma and touched his feet in respect, Gandhi, out of humility requested that these gestures not occur. Gandhi was discouraged that people were saying that the times with the British government in control in India had been much better than the current situation. He decided to fast until there was a "reunion of hearts of all communities" in Delhi. Jinnah sent a message to Gandhi to live and continue to work for Hindu-Muslim unity in India and Pakistan.

Then in Punjab's Gujaret train station hundreds of Hindus and Sikhs were maimed or killed. In Delhi 20,000 signatures were obtained with a commitment to the protection of Muslim rights and there was a peace march through the city. Gandhi told Mira that he thought he was on his greatest fast.

On the sixth day a delegation of 100 people representing various committees came to the shriveled Gandhi with a declaration stating that the faith, life and property of Muslims would be protected. There were many other pleas for Gandhi to end the fast and he finally agreed based on a commitment to nonviolence. At this time Gandhi's prestige nationally and internationally had never been higher.

At the same time, however, there was a conspiracy being planned to assassinate Gandhi by a conservative Hindu group. They felt that Gandhi's sympathy for Muslims had weakened the Hindu society. They were also angry about his support of the untouchables and were jealous of his power and popularity. First they detonated an explosion during one of his prayer meetings. Gandhi was uninjured and he calmed the crowd with great poise. He, however, continued to refuse having any police at his prayer meetings. On Friday January 30 Gandhi was heading to his prayer meeting when Natharam Godse pulled out his pistol and shot Mahatma twice in the chest and once in the stomach. The Father of the Indian nation died in the arms of his supporters but his legacy of nonviolence, freedom and love lives on.

Nelson Rolihlahla Mandela

July 18, 1918

Mvezo was a tiny village on the banks of the Mbashe River in Transkei, South Africa. This was the home of Nosekeni Fanny who was the third of four wives of Gadla Hendry Mandela. She had her thatched huts (rondavels), her farmland and livestock. On July 18, 1918 Nosekeni delivered her son who was named Rolihlahla by his father. Rolihlahla literally meant "Pulling the branch off a tree" or colloquially "trouble maker." In years to come Nelson Mandela was to make considerable trouble throughout his life for those who oppressed black Africans in his country. Transkei was a vast land between the Cape and Natal, the home of the Xhosa nation. Mandela's Xhosa ancestral roots were in the Thembu people and the Madiba clan. Mandela would later be addressed by many as Madiba, a respected term. His father was a respected chief in Thembuland and was a custodian of Xhosa history. Mandela's father

Thatched huts (rondavels)

was outspoken against situations which he found unfair. When Mandela was one year of age his father was found guilty of insubordination in a dispute with a white magistrate. For this, his chieftainship, cattle, land and income were taken from him. This led to Mandela's mother and family (three sisters and him) moving to the nearby village of Qunu where they had support from relatives. Mandela would maintain his tribal roots including building a dwelling in Qunu later in life.

Chief Jongintaba, Thembu Regent

Mandela grew up running in the veld (bush) and relating to all four "mothers," and his twelve "brothers and sisters." At five, Mandela became a herd boy looking after sheep and cattle in the fields. His birth mother became a Christian and had Mandela baptized a Methodist. Although no one in his family had had a formal education, the men of the church felt Mandela had promise and should be educated. On his first day of school his English teacher gave him the name Nelson. In 1927 Mandela's father died, probably from pulmonary tuberculosis. During his prolonged illness, he had asked his friend Chief Jongintaba, the Thembu regent, to take care of Mandela. Jongintaba was a just and powerful leader who was a committed Methodist. Mandela lived with Jongintaba's son Justice who was four years older and much more outgoing. In Mahekezweni, the regent's Great Place, Mandela learned about the great Xhosa heroes and ubuntu philosophy- one's humanity derives from how he interacts with other

Mandela at Clarkebury

people. As regent, Jongintaba listened to complaints without interruption and then developed a consensus, a style Mandela would adopt as an adult. At sixteen, Mandela underwent the circumcision ceremony which declared him a man.

Shortly after his initiation, Mandela was admitted to Clarkebury, the oldest Wesleyan mission and largest educational center in Thembuland. The regent introduced the young Mandela to the governor, Reverend Cecil Harris, who warmly shook his hand. This was the first white hand that Mandela had ever shook. Harris hired Mandela to work in his garden, since manual work was a mandatory requirement for Clarkebury. This led to Mandela's love of gardening and growing vegetables which became a comfort to him during his 27 years of imprisonment. At Clarkebury he excelled academically, completing his junior certificate in two years rather than three.

After Clarkebury Mandela enrolled at Healdtown, a Wesleyan college in Fort Beaufort, some 150 miles from the regent's Great Place. This led to continuation of his English and Methodist education which emphasized strict ethical standards and mental discipline. After graduating from Healdtown at age 21 he enrolled in Fort Hare, the only black university in South Africa. Fort Hare was the center of black intelligentsia and many of his friends were politically active. It was there that he met Oliver Tambo with whom he developed a legendary friendship.

Oliver Tambo

At Fort Hare Mandela first became active in student body activities. He fought successfully to have freshman represented on his house committee. During his second year he was supposed to run for the Student Representative Council. Before the election the students complained about the bland food and threatened to boycott the election unless the administration responded to their complaints. With no response from the administration, only 25 students voted and Mandela was one of the six elected. All 6 tendered their registration to the principal, Dr. Alexander Kerr. Kerr announced a second ballot and the results were the same; with fear of being expelled all but Mandela agreed to serve on the Student Council. Kerr indicated that Mandela would only be accepted for his final year if he agreed to serve on the Student Council. Mandela took his final exams and then went home to tell the regent that he had been expelled.

Regent Jongintaba was furious and told Mandela to return to Fort Hare at the beginning of the new term. Before that time occurred, however, the ailing regent had selected, according to Xhosa custom, a woman from a respected family to be Mandela's wife. Mandela, however, rejected this decision, since he felt love could not be bought. He therefore fled to Johannesburg, although he regretted leaving his regent

Walter Sisulu

benefactor. With the help of the regent's son, Justice, Mandela obtained a job as a night watchman at the Crown Gold Mines in Johannesburg. He slept in one of the crowded mine hostels. The regent tracked down Mandela and Justice at the gold mine, had the foreman fire them, and then ordered them to come home. Justice had also rejected an arranged marriage, so neither complied with the regent's demand. While seeking employment a relative referred Mandela to an estate agency co-headed by Walter Sisulu. Sisulu was a Xhosa even though his father was white. He was well regarded as a businessman in the black community. When Mandela told Sisulu that he desired to become a lawyer, Sisulu took him to a white legal firm where he was employed as a clerk. One of the partners at the firm, Lazar Sidelsky, generously loaned Mandela 50 pounds and gave him a suit which he wore for five years until it was threadbare. Mandela then enrolled in the University of South Africa to complete his undergraduate degree by correspondence. Mandela found housing in Alexandra which was five and a half miles from Johannesburg and where Xhosas, Sothos, Zulus, and Swazis lived. The village was known as the Dark City because it had no electricity. Mandela's room was a corrugated iron shack on the back of a house. There was a dirt floor, no running water and Mandela studied by candlelight.

During 1942 Mandela moved from Alexandra to Orlando where he was close to a house which Walter Sisulu shared with his mother. There activists and African National Congress (ANC) members came for Ma-Sisulu's cooking and political discussions. Mandela, however, focused on his education, obtained his bachelor of arts (BA) degree and enrolled in the University of Witwatersrand to pursue a law degree. Only a few blacks were admitted and they were barred from the white living quarters and sports facilities. There Mandela met Joe Slovo and Slovo's future wife, Ruth First, both avid communists and anti-racists. During his time at Witwatersrand he had a job to support himself, frequently walked

Mandela at Witwatersrand

Mandela's first wife, Evelyn Mase

several miles to class to save money, studied and attended part-time lectures. He then met Sisulu's attractive cousin, Evelyn Mase, and married her. On this demanding background, he failed his final exams and his professor refused to accept Mandela's appeal to retake the exams. So he left Witwatersrand without a law degree. Mandela and Evelyn found a matchbox house in Orlando and one year later they had a son, Mandiba Themekile (Thembi), and then a daughter, Makaziwe, in another year.

In Johannesburg Mandela experienced racial prejudice, and his first political action came in August 1943. With 10,000 others they protested the rise in bus fares. Walter Sisulu, a staunch member of the ANC, was involved and would play a pivotal role in shaping Mandela's political ideals. He, Oliver Tambo, and Mandela became Executive Members of the newly founded ANC Youth League. Later there was a miners' strike for better working conditions, but it was put down brutally by the police of Jan Smuts' government including five

Dr. Alfred Xuma

deaths and hundreds of injuries. The members of the ANC Youth League were disappointed with the old guard of the ANC. Under the leadership of Dr. Alfred Xuma a general strike to support the miners was not called. In 1947 Mandela quit the law firm so as to attempt to finish his law degree. At the same time Evelyn took maternity leave and also lost her salary so the Mandelas had to obtain a loan from the Institute of Race Relations. Then tragedy struck with newly born Makaziwe dying nine months after her birth.

In the next election the National Party gained power and invoked even stricter segregation of the races with tactics mimicking Nazi Germany. The ANC Youth League responded with a program of mass action which the old guard of the ANC did not support. This led to the removal of Dr. Xuma as ANC President by a vote of no-confidence in 1949 and Sisulu, Tambo, and Mandela were added to the ANC Executive Committee. On May 1, 1950 half of the black workers in Johannesburg went on strike. That evening the police opened fire on strikers in Orlando, Alexandra and Sophiatown. Eighteen were killed and many were wounded. The ANC's national conference in December 1951 demanded repeal of the unjust racial laws invoked by the National Party. The ANC resolution was rejected immediately by the Prime Minister. At the ANC Conference Mandela supported a united black front of Africans, Indians, and Colored and received a resounding ovation.

With the rejection of their conference resolution the ANC began to organize their mass action plan, the so-called Defiance Campaign, which followed the Ghandian nonviolence approach. The campaign included breaking racist laws by entering White Only toilets, railroad cars, restaurants and queues. Prior to these nonviolent protests the ANC had alerted the police. The second stage of the campaign envisioned protest marches, strikes and industrial actions. On the first night of the campaign, Mandela was arrested for supporting those who were breaking the curfew laws. He spent two days in a squalid jail cell and then was released without charges. This was Mandela's first incarceration. Over the next five months five thousand protestors were arrested. During this time Mandela drove around the country encouraging protestors and recruiting new ANC members. At the same time he was studying for his law degree which he eventually received. With his law degree Mandela became employed by H.M. Basner who supported his Defiance Campaign activities. Mandela became very active with his legal work, but on July 30, 1952 police arrived at his law firm with a warrant for his arrest. This was a part of a national police operation to arrest a group of ANC and Indian Congress leaders. The accused were given bail and a court hearing was set for September. In the meantime Mandela was setting up his own law practice. At the trial ANC president Moroka, to everyone's dismay, stated that he did not believe in equality of blacks and whites and that he did not wish to be associated with communism. Nevertheless he and all other defendants were found guilty of statutory communism and sentenced to nine months of hard labor, a sentence suspended for five years. Further, Mandela and fifty others were banned for six months. This included restriction to Johannesburg, prohibition of attending gatherings of any type, and not being in the company of more than one person at a time. The ANC conference which Mandela was unable to attend replaced Moroka as president with Chief Albert Luthuli. In November Oliver Tambo joined Mandela in his law practice and the firm was known as Mandela and Tambo - the first and only law firm in South Africa made up solely of black African lawyers. They were excellent partners - Mandela had his charismatic courtroom talents while Tambo was quiet and calm. They were the first choice and last resort for black people. They were inundated with work relating to the injustices of apartheid by the National Party regime. Their legal fees were modest, but the sheer volume led to improved income, and like his regent, Mandela became very well dressed with the purchase of several suits. He and Evelyn had their second son, Makgatho (Kgatho), and their third child who was named Makaziwe (Maki) after their deceased daughter. There was, however, strain in their marriage because of his many political activities. Three months after the expiration of Mandela's first banning he received a second banning. He then began thinking that the nonviolent approach was becoming ineffective. At a speech in Freedom Square in Johannesburg he told the crowd to prepare for a violent era in the fight for their freedom. For this he was censored by the ANC.

On June 26, 1955, a Congress of the People was held in Soweto demanding human rights. The Freedom Charter was developed which stated equal rights for all South Africans. The government rejected the Charter and considered it supporting socialism and communism.

THE FREEDOM CHARTER

Preamble: South Africa belongs to all who live in it, black and white and no government can justly claim authority unless it is based on the will of the people.

1. The people shall govern!
2. All national groups shall have equal rights!
3. The people shall share in the country's wealth!
4. The land shall be shared among those who work it!
5. All shall be equal before the law!

6. All shall enjoy equal human rights!
7. There shall be work and security!
8. The doors of learning and culture shall be opened!
9. There shall be houses, security and comfort!
10. There shall be peace and friendship!

In September Mandela traveled to the small town of Villiers in his Oldsmobile. On arrival he was met by police who served him a two year ban which restricted him to the Johannesburg magisterial district. This order also forced him to resign from the ANC. His speech to the Transvaal ANC therefore was read on his behalf and was known as "No Easy Walk to Freedom." It ended by stating that destroying tyranny was the highest aspiration of every free man. Mandela organized protests against the forced removal of Africans from Sophiatown, but these protests were brutally suppressed by the state police. The black Africans were moved into ghettos. The Bantu Education Act further downgraded black education.

Police using batons to suppress a crowd at Sophiatown

At home Evelyn had become a Jehovah's Witness, distributed The Watchtower, and wanted Mandela to accept her faith. She also challenged him about purported extramarital affairs which infuriated him. Mandela continued his boxing, which he had started as a youth, to relieve stress and would frequently take his oldest boy, Thembi, with him to his workouts. Evelyn issued an ultimatum for him to quit the ANC,

Mandela boxing

which he rejected. He decided to take a vacation back to Transkei where he had not been for 14 years - he was now 38 years old. He felt it was important to nurture his roots and visit his mother in Qunu.

In March 1956 Mandela received a five year ban and on December 5, 1956 he was arrested on a charge of high treason. There were charges against 156 people for planning to overthrow the government and the charges went back four years. After 4 days in jail, bail was granted and the trial set for

January 1957. When Mandela was released and returned home Evelyn had left and taken the children with her. Separation from his children was very painful for Mandela. One day, however, he noticed a beautiful young woman at the bus stop and later was introduced to her by Adelaide Tsukudu, who was to become Oliver Tambo's wife. For Mandela it was love at first sight with Nomzamo Winifred (Winnie) Mandikizela, the woman at the bus stop. Winnie came from a powerful family, was bright and became the first black social worker at Soweto's Baragwanath Hospital. With Mandela's guidance, she

Mandela's second wife, Winnie Nomzamo Winifred Mandikizela

quickly supported the struggle for freedom and provided him with the encouragement which he had always sought, but never received, from Evelyn.

Prior to the Treason Trial the majority of the developed world believed that the liberation movement in South Africa was by a bunch of extreme communists. The Treason Trial exposed that South African myth and the immoral oppression of the blacks by the National government which could no longer be seen as the protector of civilization and Christianity. The accused met evening after evening with statesmen, church people and non-governmental representation and they became seen as heroes fighting for their freedom.

There was a turn in the Treason Trial when the court removed the charges against many of the accused. Also during that time Winnie delivered a daughter, Zenani (Zeni), Mandela's mother came to help and his sister who was a nurse also lived with them. Their home life was very happy. Mandela's children with Evelyn were now being educated in Tranksei. In August 1959 the Treason Trial restarted, this time only against thirty of the original 156 accused. During a court adjournment in the Old Synagogue the news of the massacre in Sharpeville was heard. The Pan African Congress (PAC), organized by the black Africans to be less inclusive, had planned a protest to upstage the forthcoming ANC anti-pass campaign. In Sharpeville some 50 miles south of Johannesburg sixty people were killed and 180 wounded. The killings were condemned internationally as evidence of the National Party racial policies.

The massacre at Sharpeville (top)
The funeral for the victims of the Sharpeville massacre (lower)

On May 26, 1960, Luthuli, President of the ANC, burned his pass and Mandela did the same at his home in Orlando. This was followed in May 28, 1960 by a nationwide stay-at-home protest.

Mandela burning his pass

The National government then called a state of emergency and began arresting activists. Oliver Tambo, however, had been driven across the border to Botswana to maintain the ANC in exile. On May 30, 1960 six security police ransacked Mandela's home and arrested him. More than two thousand activists were arrested around the country.

After 36 hours in prison Mandela and the other defendants were taken to Pretoria for their Treason Trial. The defendants were facing ten year prison sentences. Of interest, a prison guard was allowed to take Mandela from Pretoria to Johannesburg to close his law office where he also met with Winnie privately. After five months of the trial the defense counsel withdrew because of restrictions on access to their clients. This left the defense in the hands of two accused lawyers, Mandela and Duma Nokuwe. Winnie, who was pregnant with their second child, was allowed visit Mandela with their daughter Zenani. These were stressful times emotionally and financially for the Mandela family. During the trial Mandela was allowed in the prison yard where he played with his dog, Khrushchev. On April 8, 1960 based on the

Mandela and Krushchev

Suppression of Communism Act, both the ANC and PAC were banned. In August 1960 the state of emergency was lifted so Mandela returned home and was there for Winnie giving birth to their second daughter who was named Zindziswa (Zindzi).

After the Christmas holiday the trial resumed. It was decided that if Mandela was found guilty he would go to prison, but if found innocent he would go underground on behalf of the ANC. To the surprise of the accused, the three judges handed down a verdict of the accused as not guilty. They could not prove either that the ANC had a policy of violence or was communist. The trial had lasted four years. Mandela was free for the first time since 1956. His underground existence involved moving around the country to visit clandestine ANC branches. He was becoming the voice of the people, more popular in his underground existence than before. He adopted many disguises, then there was a warrant for his arrest by the government. An ANC stay-at-home

Mandela as Defense Lawyer for the Treason Trial

national protest lasted only one day. Mandela then concluded that the National government would crush by force the nonviolent struggle for freedom. At an ANC meeting Mandela finally proposed to establish a military wing but his proposal was defeated. Mandela next took the proposal to a meeting of the Executives of the ANC, Indian Congress, Congress of Trade Unions and Colored People Congress. After an all night debate, a military organization, separate from the ANC, was formed, Umkhonto-we Sizwe (MK) - Spear of the Nation - with Mandela as Commander-in-Chief. Mandela was moving from place to place, posed as a chauffeur in a white uniform and was reading books about various people's revolutions. The newspapers dubbed Mandela the Black Pimpernel, a reference to the fictional Scarlet Pimpernel in Orczy's novel of the French Revolution, and this made him more famous. At one stage Mandela took a gardener's disguise and moved to a farm in Rivonia where he was occasionally visited by Winnie and the children. This was a great danger because the security police had her

Mandela in disguise as the Black Pimpernel

under surveillance. At night meetings the MK planned their first targets on buildings which symbolized apartheid rule - such pass offices, military installations and communications facilities. Efforts were made to avoid civilian targets. On December 16, 1960, just six days after the ANC President Luthuli received the Nobel Peace Prize, the first explosions occurred in Johannesburg, Durban, and Port Elizabeth. At that time the relationship between the ANC and MK was not known publically.

Early in 1961 the ANC received an invitation to the Pan African Conference in Addis Ababa in Ethiopia. Mandela was chosen as the ANC representative and at age 42 he had never been out of South Africa. During the next six months he would visit twelve African states before visiting Oliver Tambo in London. During his visits he spoke to heads of state, explained the ANC position, and requested support with funds, arms and military training. In Algeria Mandela was impressed with advice from a military commander who said that the goal of guerilla warfare was not to overthrow the enemy but to bring them to the negotiating table. Before returning to South Africa he received eight weeks of military training in Addis Ababa. In his absence the Nationalists were pushing a Sabotage Bill through parliament which would have the death penalty for those found guilty.

On his return to South Africa Mandela was arrested when driving from

Mandela in Kaross dress

Natal, where he visited Luthuli, to Johannesburg. He was charged with leaving the country without a passport and his trial was set for October 1962. On the first day of the trial he wore his Kaross dress to emphasize the historic nature of the struggle for freedom. The crowd clenched their fists and shouted the Xhosa word for power - "Amandla." Mandela's opening statement was as follows,

Many years ago, when I was a boy brought up in my village in the Transkei, I listened to the Elders of the tribe telling stories about the good old days, before the arrival of the white man. Then our people lived peacefully, under the democratic rule of their kings and their amapakati, and moved freely and confidently up and down the country without let or hindrance. Then the country was ours, in our own name and right …

Why is it that in this courtroom I am facing a white magistrate, confronted by a white prosecutor, escorted by white orderlies? Can anybody honestly and seriously suggest that in this type of atmosphere the scales of justice are evenly balanced? Why is it that no African in the history of this country has ever had the honor of being tried by his own kind, by his own flesh and blood…? I am a black man in a white man's court. This should not be.

During the two week trial he questioned the legitimacy of the unjust laws that drove him to desperate measures. The judge sentenced him to five years in prison in Pretoria. After six months he was handcuffed and with three other political prisoners was taken on a 15 hour trip to Cape Town docks where they boarded an old boat to Robben Island. Through the boat's portholes the guards took turns urinating on them. A few weeks later he was brought back to Pretoria where the entire MK high command had been captured. In October 1962 Mandela and colleagues were charged with sabotage and the state requested the death penalty. The prosecutors were poorly prepared and on one occasion the judge dismissed the indictment, but the accused were immediately rearrested. The so-called Rivonia Trial was to become known worldwide. At that time Winnie was on a two-year banning sentence and therefore initially was not allowed to attend the trial. Eventually the Minister of Justice allowed for her to attend as long as she did not wear traditional dress, even though the same government was encouraging Africans to embrace their culture. The interrogation of the accused always involved the threat of being hanged. The prosecution's case was closed at the end of February 1964. The defendants, led by Mandela, decided not to testify but to make a statement about how the National legislation had taken away the blacks "dignity, destroyed their family life and shredded their society."

> During my lifetime I have dedicated myself to this struggle of the African people. I have fought against white domination, and I have fought against black domination. I have cherished the ideal of a democratic and free society in which all persons live together in harmony and with equal opportunities. It is an ideal which I hope to live for and to achieve. But if needs be, it is an ideal for which I am prepared to die.

All night vigils were held at St. Paul's Cathedral in London in support of the accused and a United Nations Security Council resolution was passed urging cessation of the trial and granting of amnesty for the defendants. The United States and Great Britain abstained from the resolution. Mandela and the other accused were found guilty on all counts. They expected the death penalty but there was a roar from the court room when they then were flown to the prison on Robben Island.

Mandela's cell at Robben Island

At that time Mandela was 46 years old and a political prisoner with a life sentence. He and the other prisoners were given prison uniforms and placed in very small, cold damp cells. His bedding was a mat on the concrete floor with blankets. When he stretched out, his feet almost touched the opposite cell walls. He was in fairly good health but did have high blood pressure. Mandela began by protesting the short pants given the prisoners. When offered long pants, which his fellow prisoners did not receive he returned them. Three years later he and his fellow prisoners received long pants.

The quarry at Robben Island

Mandela was given his prison number 466/64 because he was the 466th prisoner incarcerated in 1964. As a political prisoner he could only send and receive one letter every six months, the length of which was limited to 500 words. Mandela cherished the biannual letters and wrote, "A letter was like summer rain that could make even the desert bloom." Two months after Mandela's arrival on Robben Island, Winnie was able to visit him for 30 minutes. It was two years before he was able to see Winnie again.

Prisoners in rows smashing stones

The work in the prison consisted of smashing stones into gravel for roads with a five pound hammer. The prisoners sat in rows, were allowed no breaks and were not allowed to talk. In the winter the yard was cold and in the summer the prisoners baked in the sun. The work day ended at 4:00 pm. They then showered in brackish cold water and only after eight years could they bathe in warm water. The prisoners ate in their cells; the food was corn porridge, soggy pieces of vegetable and every other day a gristly piece of meat. On weekends the prisoners were locked in their cells except for a daily one hour exercise break. Sleep time was 8:00 pm unless permission to study was obtained. Mandela was permitted to continue to study law during the evening.

In spite of these harsh circumstances Mandela never believed that he would die behind bars and his optimism was felt by his fellow prisoners. In 1965 the stone breaking was replaced by the more grueling work in the lime quarry. The prisoners had to break through stone to reach the lime which was then dug out with pick and shovels. The prisoners were told that their work in the lime quarry would last six months, but it carried on for thirteen years. There was blinding sun and the prisoners were initially not allowed to have sunglasses. After three years they were allowed to buy their own sunglasses. However, by that time the eyesight of Mandela and others had been irreparably damaged. When the International Red Cross came to the Robben Island Prison Mandela was allowed to meet with a representative alone. He requested that the prisoners receive proper clothing including pants, socks, and underwear. He complained about the food, infrequent letters and visitors, the labor in the lime quarry, and mistreatment by the guards. As a result of this Red Cross meeting, however, nothing changed.

In July 1966 a hunger strike started in the main section of the prison in protest of the disgraceful conditions. In solidarity the political prisoners in Mandela's group joined in the hunger strike. During the hunger strike Winnie was allowed to visit Mandela. He knew from newspapers available to him that Winnie had undergone constant harassment by the security police. His thirty minutes with her through the smudged sun glass showed that she was thin and drawn. They discussed Mandela's mother's health, the girls' education, and their poor financial situation.

In addition to the International Red Cross, the only opposition member of Parliament, Helen Suzman of the Progressive Party, visited Mandela and heard about the prisoner's complaints. She then began to work to improve conditions in the prison. In the spring of 1968 Mandela's mother visited for the first time. She came from Transkei with his son Makgatho and daughter Makazwe and her sister Mabel. They were only allowed forty-five minutes to visit. A few weeks later Mandela heard that his mother had died of a heart attack. His request to attend her funeral was denied. Mandela's fortitude was to be tested further in May 1969 when Winnie was arrested under the Terrorism Act and placed in solitary confinement in Pretoria. Three months later Mandela's mental torture worsened when Makgatho sent him a telegram about Thembi's death in a car accident. His request to attend the funeral was denied.

In the 1970's the prisoners were allowed to have vegetable gardens. Mandela had been requesting this privilege for years. His garden produced tomatoes, chilies, radishes, onions and sweet melons which he shared with the other prisoners and even the guards. He wrote secretly in a manuscript that "the sense of being the custodian of this small patch of earth offered a small taste of freedom." Fellow prisoners, Walter Sisulu and Ahmed Kathrada, encouraged Mandela to write his autobiography. It was felt that Mac Maharaj, who was due to be released in 1976 after serving 12 years for sabotage, could smuggle the manuscript out of the prison to be published in 1978 on Mandela's 60th birthday. For four months Mandela worked every night on the manuscript, which was transcribed in a minute script the next day by Maharaj on thin sheets of paper to be hidden in his study materials. The original 500 page manuscript was then placed in plastic cocoa containers and buried in three different places in the garden. Unfortunately the authorities found one of the containers which resulted in the study privileges of Mandela, Sisulu, and Kathrada being taken away for four years. Maharaj, however, smuggled out his copy, but it was 18 years before the manuscript was published as "Long Walk to Freedom."

Shortly after completing his manuscript Mandela heard that Winnie had been released from prison and her banning order had expired. Winnie and their 15 year old daughter, Zindzi, whom Mandela had not seen since she was three years old, were able to visit. Zindzi had the beauty and fire of her mother. During the visit all were challenged to hold back their tears.

The Soweto riots

In 1974 the National government made Afrikaans the language for educating pupils from the seventh grade forward. In protest on June 16, 1976 thousands of youths in Soweto marched in protest to this rule. The police opened fire on the protestors and 600 children were shot and many were killed. Over the next two years Soweto became a battleground of children throwing stones against police who used automatic rifles, tear gas, armored vehicles and helicopters to attack the protestors. Hundreds of youths were jailed and others escaped to join the MK. In support Mandela smuggled out a message in support of the protestors:

> We who are confined within the grey walls of the Pretoria regime's prisons reach out to our people. With you we count those who have perished by means of the gun and the hangman's rope. We salute all of you - the living, the injured, and the dead. For you have dared to rise up against the tyrant's might .... We face the future with confidence for the guns that serve apartheid cannot render it conquerable. Those who live by the gun shall perish by the gun.
>
> Unite! Mobilize! Fight on!
>
> Between the anvil of united mass action and the hammer of the armed struggle we shall crush apartheid and white minority racist rule.
>
> Amandla!

While on Robben Island no pictures were taken of Mandela so he was still mysterious to the public. While he was at the Clinic for treatment of tuberculosis and later at Victor Verster Prison, he was offered from 500,000-1,000,000 rand from news outlets to allow his picture to be taken. He refused, stating that he did not want to benefit personally from his freedom struggle for all of South Africa.

In the 1980's Mandela sensed changes in support of the freedom fight in South Africa. He was awarded the Jawaharlal Nehru Human Rights Award in India. Oliver Tambo initiated a Free Mandela campaign in London, which was taken up by the Johannesburg newspaper, The Sunday World. The new prime minister, P.W. Botha, was against freeing Mandela but on March 31, 1982 Mandela, Sisulu, and two others were suddenly moved to Pollsmoor Prison in Tokei, a suburb 18 miles from Capetown. Ahmed Kathrada joined them a few months later. There were proper beds, improved food, and access to the radio, newspapers, and magazines. Mandela, however, missed the discussions and teachings on Robben Island which had led to their group being named the "university." Access to Mandela at Pollsmoor Prison, however, increased substantially and again he cultivated a garden. Botha introduced a tricamaral parliament with separate houses for whites, coloreds, and Indians. Mandela was against this approach which excluded black Africans. His freedom struggle was for a unified South Africa with equality for all.

> "Only free men can negotiate. Prisoners cannot enter into contracts. I cannot and will not give any undertaking at a time when I and you, the people, are not free. Your freedom and mine cannot be separated. I will return."

Mandela was disappointed with Botha's non-aggressive pact with Mozambique, particularly after his old friend Ruth First, who was Joe Slovo's wife, was assassinated by a letter bomb in the capital city of Maputo. Other ANC operatives also were assassinated in Maputo for which in response the MK exploded a car bomb outside the Pretoria office of the South African Air Force. Nineteen people were killed and two hundred injured. Mandela regretted the escalation in violence, however he thought this was inevitable given the government's attacks and assassinations inside and outside the country. In May 1984 at Pollsmoor Prison he had his first contact visit with Winnie in 21 years, they embraced and kissed.

Mandela's daughter Zindzi reading his rejection of Botha's proposal

The international anti-apartheid intensity against South Africa was growing with sports boycotts, economic boycotts, academic boycotts, and arms embargos. There were discussions about conditionally releasing Mandela and other prisoners to Transkei, a Bantustan, where blacks would live separately from whites. This separation was immediately rejected by Mandela and his fellow prisoners; their goal was to have a unified South Africa. Mandela released his statement of rejection of Botha's proposal which was read by his daughter Zindzi to a packed stadium. These were his first words heard in public for more than two decades. The violence continued and the government called a state of emergency on July 20, 1985 which gave the security police draconian powers to torture and assassinate. The state of emergency, however, brought dire economic consequences against South Africa - international banks withdrew credit, the exchange rate plummeted, some international companies withdrew their products and calls for further economic sanctions increased. It became clear that only Mandela's release could prevent anarchy and civil war. In the midst of all this turmoil Mandela had prostate surgery. The next government proposal was to conditionally release Mandela if he would renounce violence. The response letter drafted by Mandela was also signed by Sisulu, Kathrada, Andrew Mlangeni and Raymond Mblaba from Pollsmoor Prison to P.W. Botha stated the following steps must be taken by the government:

1. Violence must be renounced;
2. Apartheid must be dismantled;
3. ANC must be unbanned;
4. All who have been imprisoned, banished or exiled because of their opposition to apartheid must be freed;
5. Free political activity must be guaranteed.

Some disturbing events then occurred in Soweto with Winnie. She formed for protection the Mandela United Football Club which turned into a murderous vigilante gang. Mandela asked Winnie to disband the group but she refused. Also during 1988 the violence in the townships continued. However, the support for Mandela worldwide continue to increase. In July a pop concert was held in London's Wembly Stadium for thousands to celebrate Mandela's seventieth birthday and it was broadcast worldwide. He was becoming a figure of mythic dimensions. Moreover, Botha had agreed to meet with him in August. However, a battle between Winnie's gang and a rival gang led to Mandela's house in Orlando being set on fire and family papers and letters were destroyed. Public sentiment in Soweto turned against Winnie.

Then Mandela became ill and was diagnosed with tuberculosis which led to a four month hospitalization and cancellation of the Botha meeting. Mandela recuperated at a Clinic not far from the Pollsmoor Prison where he had a view of the mountains and an exercise bike which he used aggressively. There his contacts with the Minister of Justice Coetsee resumed. In December 1988 he was discharged from the Clinic and driven to Victor Verster Prison where he was to live in a white house shaded by pine trees with an excellent kitchen and chef. The garden was large and there was a swimming pool. Minister Coetsee called in the afternoon with a case of excellent wine. He assured Mandela that here they could have discussions in privacy and comfort. At the house in Victor Verster, Jack Swart, was the Warden Officer guarding Mandela and cooking for him. One day Mandela told Swart that he would wash the dishes. The guard disagreed but Mandela insisted. They became good friends and Mandela invited Swart to his presidential inauguration.

Mandela's triumphant release from prison, with Winnie at his side

In January Winnie's gang continued to terrorize. She watched while a boy was accused of being an informer and was beaten. Later his severed head was found in a riverbed. A group, the Mandela Crisis Committee, was formed to confront Winnie. Mandela was quite distressed and wanted to believe in his wife's innocence. In the same month Botha had a stroke and his meeting with Mandela was again postponed. In July, however, they finally met at the presidential residence. The meeting was cordial, however, Botha refused Mandela's request for the political prisoners to be released. However, in the last quarter of the year F.W. de Klerk was elected president and in October the Robben Island contingent, including Sisulu and Kathrada. Two months later de Klerk met with Mandela who felt that the ANC could negotiate with him. February 2, 1990 de Klerk announced the unbanning of the ANC, PAC, and the Communist Party. Seven days later de Klerk told Mandela that he would be released that weekend in Johannesburg. Mandela indicated that he needed a week to prepare and desired to leave from the Victor Verster Prison. de Klerk indicated that the date could not be changed but Mandela could leave from the prison. Thus, on Sunday, February 11, 1990 at 4:00 pm after nearly three decades in prison, Nelson Mandela with Winnie walked through the prison gate. Mandela refused to leave prison without Winnie by his side. His life he felt was just beginning anew. In "Long Walk to Freedom," he said, "I always knew that someday I would once again feel the grass under my feet and walk in the sunshine a free man."

His ten thousand days of imprisonment had ended. A huge crowd of well-wishers, journalists, photographers, and television cameras awaited Mandela as he emerged. He had a broad smile and raised his hand in the ANC salute. The crowd roared "Amandla." Mandela then went to the Cape Town's Grand Parade where he spoke from the balcony of City Hall.

Speaking from Cape Town City Hall

Friends, comrades, and fellow South Africans. I greet you all in the name of peace, democracy, and freedom for all. I stand here before you not as a prophet but as a humble servant of you, the people. Your tireless and heroic sacrifices have made it possible for me to be here today. I therefore place the remaining years of my life in your hands.

February 11, 1990
Cape Town City Hall

He further said, "We have waited too long for our freedom. We can wait no longer. Now is the time to intensify the struggle on all fronts." Mandela spent

Bishop Desmond Tutu and Mandela

his first night of freedom in the residence of Archbishop Desmond Tutu and the next day he and Winnie flew to Johannesburg. The next day he spoke to approximately 100,000 people in Soweto.

> Comrades, friends, and the people of Soweto at large, I greet you in the name of the heroic struggle of our people to establish justice and freedom for all in our country.

Orlando, where Winnie and Nelson Mandela lived

They then returned to their home in Orlando which had been rebuilt.

From the moment Mandela left prison Winnie would not enter his bedroom until he was asleep. His relations with his children were also strained. Months later when his daughter Makaziwe (Maki, second daughter with Evelyn) returned from a stay in Canada, Mandela tried to hug her but she moved away and said, "You are a father to all of our people but you never had the time to be a father to me." Zenani (Zeni, first daughter with Winnie) said, "From the day my father was free, we had to share him with the rest of the world." His friends, however, found him warm and gentle, more at peace than the angry young man who went to prison.

One of Mandela's first challenges after his release from prison was an attempt to halt the violence in Kwa Zulu-Natal. Chief Mangosuthu Buthelezi controlled the Inkatha Freedom Party of Zulus which was fighting for power in the area against the ANC. Three weeks after his release Mandela flew to Durban where he saw grieving families and burnt corpses of ANC supporters. He addressed a crowd of about 100,000, mainly Zulus, and told them," Take your guns, your knives, your pangos and throw them into the sea. Close down the death factories. End this war now." Unfortunately the killings continued. There was substantial evidence that elements of the government were encouraging violence against the ANC by the Inkatha Freedom Party and colored voters in the Cape.

There was agreement on talks with the National government to start in April. But on March 26 in Seboko Township near Johannesburg, police opened fire on an ANC demonstration and killed 12 with hundreds wounded. In protest Mandela suspended the planned talks. When talks later were started de Klerk tried to have Mandela speak out against the international economic sanctions on South Africa. Mandela refused and said only after apartheid is dismantled. Mandela had moved into Winnie's seven bedroom house in Soweto even though he was uncomfortable with the extravagance and stories of Winnie's heavy drinking. Mandela and Winnie then left on a six week "thank you" tour of Europe and North America to encourage increased sanctions on South Africa until apartheid was dismantled. On leaving London for the United States he spoke to British Prime Minister Margaret Thatcher who told him, "If you keep up with this hectic pace, you will not come out of America alive." However, in New York City there was a 15 mile long tickertape parade, the longest the city had seen. He spoke to a joint session of both houses of Congress. On his returning to London Thatcher indicated that she would not apply sanctions against South Africa which Mandela had requested.

On return to South Africa there was increasing violence in Kwa Zulu with 1500 deaths in July, more than the total for the previous 12 months. Then hundreds of Zulus were bussed into Sebopkong and the ANC informed the Minister of Law and Order about this development. Nevertheless, the police did not intervene. The next day Mandela saw 30 bodies in the morgue which had been hacked to death with the broad-bladed pangos. Mandela

Mandela and de Klerk

blamed de Klerk rather than Buthelezi. Three days later the security police arrested forty ANC members claiming they planned to overthrow the government. Mandela visited many townships during the atrocities and heard many stories about security police collusion with the Inkatha. While Mandela was having talks with the government and thousands had died in the Transvaal townships, the government approved a regulation that allowed Zulus to carry their cultural weapons of war, e.g. fighting sticks and axes. Mandela accused de Klerk and the security police of orchestrating the continued slaughter with the obvious goal to weaken the ANC and Mandela's leadership.

At the same time Winnie could be seen in an MK uniform supporting "shooting our way to freedom." Because of rumors of abduction and murders, Mandela had difficulty raising funds for the defense of her trial. Winnie was found guilty of kidnapping and sentenced to six years in prison. She appealed the verdict and Mandela continued to believe she was innocent. Politically, as the violence continued, newspapers in South Africa and Great Britain reported stories about security police supplying weapons to the Inkatha Freedom Party. There were also reports of death squads. Mandela became president of the ANC and official negotiations with the government began at Johannesburg World Trade Center; they were called Convention for a Democratic South Africa (CODESA1). While Winnie's appeal was underway a negative story about her behavior appeared in the Soweto newspaper and coincided with another one of her wild parties to celebrate Zindzi's engagement. Fourteen days later Mandela announced his separation from his wife. He said, "I part from my wife with no recrimination. I embrace her with all the love and affection I have nursed for her inside and outside the prison from the moment I first met her." Later came a story published in the Sunday Times of Winnie's letter to her lover and her cashing of fraudulent checks. On the political front, CODESA2 started. Then on June 17 an Inkatha war party including white men with blackened faces slaughtered 45 people in the township of Boipatong. This led to Mandela breaking off talks. During an ANC protest march in Ciskei soldiers opened fire and killed 28 people, an event strongly criticized by Mandela. In spite of the violence and great friction between Mandela and de Klerk, the conference ended with a Record of Understanding that committed the government to a constitutional assembly and a transitional Government of National Unity.

With the news of the assassination on April 10 of Chis Hani, one of the most popular black leaders and former MK commander, the country exploded. Rioting and looting left seventy dead in the Cape and Natal. Mandela then broadcast a message on national television. He said, "Tonight I am reaching out to every single South African, black and white, from the very depth of my being. A white man, full of prejudice and hate, came to our country (from Poland) and committed a deed so foul that our whole nation now teeters on the brink of disaster. A white woman of African origin who identified the killer's license plates at the risk of her life so that we may know, and bring to justice, this assassin." It was that speech that quieted the rage and turmoil of the country and made Mandela the embodiment of the future of South Africa. Two weeks later Mandela said, "I am the loneliest man in the world," because his longtime friend and colleague Oliver Tambo died. He said that it was as if part of him had died.

Next, by rallying international support, an election date of April 27, 1994 was agreed with de Klerk and the government. Mandela was saddened however by the Appeals Court upholding the charge of kidnapping against Winnie. She was given a two year suspended term of imprisonment and a $5,000 fine. The bloodshed in South Africa continued and was further ignited by the demagogue, Eugene Terrel Blank of the African Weirstand Beveging (AWB).

In the historic year of 1994 with the successes at the World Trade Center, Mandela and de Klerk were jointly awarded the Nobel Peace Prize, even though their relationship remained stormy. The violence in Kwa Zulu-Natal remained rampant between the ANC and Inkatha Freedom Party. Then

Mandela at the World Trade Center

Mandela and de Klerk sharing the Nobel Peace Prize

the massacre in Cape Town occurred with PAC gunmen bursting into a pub and killing three young women and a nearby restaurant owner.

Whites and blacks lined up in the hot sun for hours to vote in the first democratic election in South Africa

Buthelezi decided to boycott both the election and the new Constitution. Mandela and de Klerk tried to convince him to change his mind. International mediation led by Henry Kissinger and Lord Carrington also failed to convince the Zulu Chief to participate.

Mandela casts his vote

However, Kenyan Professor, Washington Okumu, convinced him to meet with Mandela and de Klerk. Mandela indicated to Buthelezi that he would a part of the government if the ANC won. Buthelezi then had a change of heart and agreed to participate just seven days before the election took place. Whites and blacks lined up in the hot sun for hours to vote in the first democratic election in South Africa. In contrast to some dire forecasts the election occurred peacefully. Mandela traveled to Durban to vote near the grave of John Dube, one of the founders of ANC 82 years earlier.

> We have struggled hard for this day. For the day when all South Africans – colored, African, Indian, and white – could together choose a government that would represent the interests of the majority of our people.

Mandela sworn in as President of South Africa

Five days later de Klerk conceded and the ANC held a joyous victory party. For the first time Mandela cried publicly with joy about his victory. He said,

"People of South Africa, this is a joyous night. I look forward to working with you for our beloved country." On May 9, 1994 Mandela was sworn in as President of South Africa. Mandela then went to the Grand Parade where four years before he had spoken after his release from prison. The following day he was inaugurated as President at Pretoria. Heads of state, signatories and celebrities had come from around the world to South Africa to offer congratulations. Mandela said, "I am simply the sum of all those African patriots who had gone before me ... I was pained that I was not able to thank them and that they were not able to see what their sacrifice had wrought." He further expressed that, "Never, never and never again shall it be that this beautiful land will experience the oppression of one by another . . . The sun shall never set on this glorious human achievement. Let freedom reign."

At his inauguration, Mandela's daughter Zendzi was at his side and Winnie was seated in the audience. Evelyn was not invited. President Mandela raised the hands of former president C.W.

Mandela celebrates his inauguration with de Klerk and Mbeki

de Klerk and future president Thabo Mbeki. As always, Mandela's great smile was captivating. Leading a Government of National Unity was a challenge for Mandela. His relations with de Klerk and Minister of Home Affairs Buthelezi were abrasive. During his five year term he traveled extensively and much of the day-to-day tasks were undertaken by Mbeki. Mandela participated in several peace efforts during his term, including Angola, Indonesia, Ireland, and the Democratic Republic of Conga (formerly Zaire). In his last month he convinced Quaddafi to surrender the men responsible for the Lockerbie bombing.

Mandela began wearing bright, loose fitting shirts which he said after 27 years in prison made him feel free. To bring the country together at the 1995 World Rugby

Mandela at the 1995 World Rugby Cup

Cup he wore a Springbok jersey in front of the largely Afrikaner crowd. A movie, Invictus, depicts how Mandela used this rugby tournament to bring white and black South Africans together. The underdog South African team won the World Cup against New Zealand 15-12.

In January 1995 Mandela learned that before the election de Klerk had granted thousands of security police indemnity from prosecution. This angered Mandela. Shortly thereafter Winnie's house was raided by the fraud squad because of allegations of illegal debts and financial mismanagement. His divorce from Winnie had brought him great sadness and then he had to remove her from his government for breaking cabinet rules. Later, however, Graça Machel, widow of the Mozambican president, entered his life.

Mandela and Graça Machel

In February 1996 Mandela launched the Truth and Reconciliation Commission which was headed by Desmond Tutu. In May the most

Mandela and Desmond Tutu with the Truth and Reconciliation Commission

progressive human rights Constitution was passed by parliament. The next day, however, de Klerk removed his party from the government. Mandela gradually withdrew from politics and at the end of 1997 he stepped down as president of the ANC. That Christmas he spent time with Graça in Qunu where he had built a house similar to his cottage at Victor Verster Prison. Later, on Mandela's eightieth birthday, they married and moved into a house in Houghton. After the June 1999 election Thabo Mbeki became president. Although much had been promised, but not all achieved, during Mandela's presidency improvements had occurred in health care, housing, electricity, clean water and land resettlement had occurred.

While Mandela claimed to be retiring, he remained committed to international peace. In South Africa he had donated a large sum from his salary to aid children's welfare and now his Children's Fund is well financed. The Mandela Rhodes Fellowship

Mandela in Qunu

Mandela with AIDS baby

Mandela with children in his Children's Fund

was launched for outstanding Africans to attend African institutions. The Nelson Mandela Foundation also became a large philanthropic institution. Mandela and Graça became fund raisers *par excellence* for these philanthropic causes. Mandela lost his son, Makatho, to AIDS and he began campaigning for HIV/AIDS awareness which was affecting millions of South Africans. This conflicted with the Mbeki government which was denying the existence of this dreaded disease. Mandela continued to write his memoirs. This was interrupted by the death of Walter Sisulu, who was his best friend and mentor. A wise, quiet and unassuming man whom was loved and respected by many, the loss of Sisulu was devastating to Mandela.

Words cannot describe how Nelson Mandela has become an icon for the world. Forging a multiracial democratic South Africa after 27 years in prison and with the oppression of apartheid appeared

Mandela in the traditional dress of the feather of the blue crane, presented to him by the Xhosa king in honor of his achievements

impossible except to Mandela and his colleagues. Mandela projected both nobility and humility and still does project this in his 90's. He was always committed to reconciliation with his previous enemies, both from a humanistic

view but also as a political strategy. Mandela's life is a unique inspiration for

the past, present, and future generations.

Martin Luther King Jr.

January 15, 1929 - April 4, 1968

Martin Luther King Jr. was born in Atlanta, Georgia on January 15, 1929 to Reverend Martin Luther King Sr. and Alberta Williams King who was a teacher. He had an older sister, Willie Christine King, and a younger brother, Alfred Williams King. With his father, grandfather and great grandfather being Baptist ministers, Martin became involved in religion at a very young age. He was a member of the church choir at 10 years old. At age 13 he even voiced skepticism during Sunday School about the physical resurrection of Jesus after his crucifixion.

At age fourteen Martin went to Dublin, Georgia to compete in an oratorical contest. His presentation was entitled, "The Negro and the Constitution," and he won. Part of his oration was the following:

> We cannot have an enlightened democracy with one great group living in ignorance. We cannot have a healthy nation with one-tenth of the people ill-nourished, sick, harboring germs of disease which recognize no color lines - obey no Jim Crow laws. We cannot have a nation orderly and sound with one group so ground down and thwarted that it is almost forced into unsocial attitudes and crime. We cannot be truly Christian people so long as we flout the central teachings of Jesus: brotherly love and the Golden Rule. We cannot come to full prosperity with one great group so ill-delayed that it cannot buy goods. So as we gird ourselves to defend democracy from foreign attack, let us see to it that increasingly at home we give fair play and free opportunity for all people.
> Today thirteen million black sons and daughters of our forefathers continue the fight for the translation of the Thirteenth, Fourteenth, and Fifteenth Amendments from writing on the printed page to an actuality. We believe with them that "if

freedom is good for any it is good for all," that we may conquer Southern armies by the sword, but it is another thing to conquer Southern hate, that if the franchise is given to Negroes, they will be vigilant and defend, even with their arms, the ark of federal liberty from reason and destruction by her enemies.

On the trip back to Atlanta white passengers boarded the bus and the white bus driven told Martin and his teacher to give their seats to the white passengers. Martin was very angry but his teacher, Mrs. Bradley, told him that they must obey the law. They therefore stood in the aisle during the ninety miles back to Atlanta.

Another memorable time in Martin's youth was when he worked on a tobacco farm in Connecticut during the summer before going to college. He went freely to the church and restaurants with his white colleagues. However, on the train back he had to switch to the car for blacks in Washington, D.C. These events had an early effect on Martin's sense of self respect and dignity. He felt that segregated schools, restaurants, waiting rooms, drinking fountains, theaters and lavatories in the South were a great injustice to colored people.

At an early stage Martin was a remarkable student. At Booker T. Washington High school he skipped the ninth and twelfth grades and entered Morehouse College at age fifteen with thoughts of becoming a lawyer or doctor. However, he was influenced by George B. Kelsey, a religion professor, and Dr. Benjamin Hayes, the college's president. Martin then better understood the social and intellectual tradition of the ministry and by graduation he had decided to pursue the ministry. He, however, became more skeptical about religious fundamentals and struggled to resolve some aspects of religion with science.

Martin graduated from Morehouse College with a Bachelor of Arts degree in sociology at the age of 19. He then entered Crozer Theological seminary in Chester, Pennsylvania. For the next three years he studied philosophy, ethics, and the religious and social views of Reinhold Niebuhr. It was during this time that he learned about the nonviolent activities of Mahandas Gandhi. At Crozer he was respected by his professors and classmates. He was elected student body president and was valedictorian of his class. He received his Bachelor of Divinity degree at age 22. On graduation he won a fellowship for graduate studies. He was accepted for doctoral studies at

King with his mentor, Gandhi

Boston University where he studied systematic theology. After completing his coursework he began his dissertation comparing the views of Paul Tillich and Henry Nelson Wierman.

When Martin was a student at Boston University he met Howard Thurman who was not only a theologian and educator but also a civil rights leader. During his missionary work abroad Thurman had met Mahatmas Gandhi and discussed Gandhi's nonviolent struggles for freedom with Martin. Thurman had a major impact on King's future civil rights activities. Another major advisor to King about his civil rights activities was Bayard Rustin. Rustin had also studied Gandhi's teachings and was the main organizer of King's 1963 Civil Rights March in Washington. However, African-American leaders later forced King to distance himself from Rustin because of Rustin's former ties with the Communist party.

Martin Luther King Jr. with his family

King met and later married Coretta Scott on June 18, 1953. She was from Marion, Alabama and had gone to Antioch College in Ohio. Coretta was a scholarship student at the New England Conservatory in Boston. Her plans were to become a concert singer until she met Martin in Boston. They married in Marion and had four children, Yolanda King, Martin Luther King III, Dexter Scott King, and Bernice King. At age 25 King became the pastor of the Dexter Avenue Baptist Church in Montgomery, Alabama. He considered some pastorships in the North, but he and Coretta felt that they could make more of a social and spiritual contribution by returning to the South. King's installation as pastor of Dexter was conducted by his father, who was pastor of Ebenezer Baptist Church in Atlanta, Georgia. During his first year he organized his congregation, completed his dissertation, and received his Doctor of Philosophy (PhD) degree from Boston University on June 5, 1955.

After the Civil War and the Emancipation Proclamation, the Jim Crow laws and the Ku Klux Klan perpetuated segregation and oppression of the former Negro slaves in the South. This included threats, beatings, and even lynchings if any African-American considered voting, tried to sit in the front of the bus, entered white only restaurants or toilets to mention a few of the vehicles of continued segregation of blacks from whites in the South.

During King's first year as a pastor in Montgomery, Rosa Parks, a seamstress and secretary of the Montgomery NAACP Chapter, refused on

December 1, 1955 to give up her seat in the front of the bus to a white customer. This was a personal decision independent of her relationship with the NAACP. Parks was found in violation of the segregated seating ordinance on public buses in Montgomery. As a result she was arrested. Black citizens were outraged and they founded the Montgomery Improvement Association to protest this

Rosa Parks

bus segregation law. King, to his surprise, was elected president of this Association because he was charismatic, a powerful orator, a clergy committed to nonviolent civil rights and was a newcomer to Montgomery who had not yet made any enemies. Ralph Abernathy, pastor of Montgomery's First Baptist Church, became vice-president and a lifelong friend of King's.

The Montgomery buses were boycotted by the blacks who constituted 70% of the bus customers. The boycott lasted 381 days during which time King's house was bombed and he was also arrested with many others. Abernathy's house and church were also bombed. King was convicted on charges of conspiring to interfere with the bus company's operations. He received multiple mail and phone death threats. During the entire boycott King preached nonviolence as espoused by Gandhi and Henry David Thoreau in

"Essay of Civil Disobedience." Initially the black-owned taxis gave the boycotters reduced fares until the city blocked that practice. Then the boycotters formed carpools. Approximately 300 cars were assembled and 42 pick up sites designated. The drivers included ministers, housewives, teachers, businessmen and unskilled laborers. Some laborers and domestic workers walked as far as twelve miles to their jobs and home again. Some men rode mules and others had horse-drawn buggies. Abernathy headed a committee for the Association which formulated their demands to end the boycott. The demands were (1) courtesy from bus drivers who had been known to call Negroes "niggers," "black apes," and "black cows"; (2) bus seats by first come, first serve; and (3) black bus drivers on primarily black routes. These demands were rejected by the Montgomery white government. Ultimately, the United States District Court ended racial segregation on all public buses in Montgomery, Alabama. The United States Supreme Court declared Alabama's segregation laws unconstitutional. King was the first to step on an integrated bus in Montgomery. As a result, at the young age of 26, King became a national civil rights hero. King wrote a book about the Montgomery bus boycott entitled, "Stride Toward Freedom."

In 1957 King, Ralph Abernathy, and 60 black ministers met in Atlanta and organized the Southern Christian Leadership Conference (SCLC). The

SCLC brought together black churches to fight nonviolently against racial segregation. King led the SCLC until he was killed in 1968. In February 1958 twenty-one mass meetings in southern cities were sponsored by the SCLC as part of the "Crusade for Citizenship." This led to a 100% increase in registered voters in the South. King continued to travel and speak at nonviolent protests against the racial injustice throughout the South. He praised President Eisenhower for using the National Guard to allow Negro students to enter Little Rock High School.

In 1959 Prime Minister Jawaharlal Nehru invited Dr. and Mrs. King to visit India. They visited Gandhi's birth place and studied his successes using nonviolent protests in India, as well as earlier in South Africa. On leaving India, King said that he was convinced that nonviolent resistance was a potent vehicle for oppressed people in their fight for justice and freedom. On return to the United States the nonviolent civil rights struggle intensified. In response there was violent and bloody resistance by whites against the peaceful black protesters. In order to have the freedom and time to pursue

Ebenezeer Baptist Church

and lead the civil rights struggle King moved from Montgomery to Atlanta to become a co-pastor with his father at the Ebenezer Baptist Church. Ralph Abernathy joined them there. Abernathy and King remained together in the civil rights struggle until the end of King's life.

In February 1960 a sit-in movement began in Greensboro, North Carolina by African-American students in protest to segregation of lunch counters. This movement then spread to South Carolina, Tennessee and Virginia. The black students frequently were joined by white civil rights protestors. In April the SCLC called a conference to help student sit-in leaders coordinate their movement. This led to the formation of the Student Nonviolent Coordinating Committee (SNCC). Initially the SCLC and the SNCC worked closely together but later there were disagreements between the groups. In February 1960 King was arrested and charged with falsifying Alabama State income tax returns. The case was tried by an all-white Southern jury and all of the State witnesses were white. After a three day trial the jury returned a verdict of acquittal.

A report in August 1960 indicated that segregation at lunch counters had ended in 27 Southern cities. In many places the students were confronted by police guns, angry whites, tear gas, arrests and jail sentences. At a segregated department store in Atlanta King and 75 students requested lunch counter service and were arrested. When King was jailed in Atlanta, Georgia, John F. Kennedy, who was campaigning for the presidency, made a call to Mrs. King and with the resultant political pressure her husband was ultimately released. This pressure involved Senator Robert Kennedy calling Georgia Governor S. Ernest Vandiver and Judge Oscar Mitchell.

In 1961 thousands of citizens in Albany, Georgia formed a desegregation coalition. This led to mass arrests of nonviolent, peaceful demonstrators including King. In July 1962 King was sentenced to 45 days in jail or pay a fine of $178.86. He chose the jail sentence. Three days later, however, the police chief Laurie Pritchett paid the fine and ordered King's release. King said, "We have been kicked off luncheon stools, ejected from churches, thrown in jail, but this is the first time that we have been kicked out of jail." Then on July 27 King and others held a prayer vigil at City Hall and were arrested again. He then was told that someone had posted his cash bond and that he could leave the jail but King refused to leave. After court hearings he and Ralph Abernathy were given suspended sentences. The "jail-ins," along with "sit-ins," "kneel-ins," and "prayer-ins," led to partial victories in Albany. The City Commission repealed the City's segregation ordinances.

Attorney General Robert F. Kennedy warned King that alleged Communist associations in SCLC could have a negative effect on his civil rights movement. Kennedy directed J. Edgar Hoover, the head of the Federal Bureau of Investigation (FBI), to begin telephone tapping King and the other SCLC leaders. No evidence of Communist infiltration in the SCLC was found, but other incriminating details about his private life were used against King as leader of the civil rights movement. The King-led nonviolent marches for blacks' right to vote, labor rights, and other basic civil rights led to public media exposure of the violence and indignities suffered by blacks. This led to substantial positive public opinion, particularly in the North, for black civil rights equality.

After King was released from jail he flew to Washington DC and met with Vice-President Herbert Humphrey who chaired the council on Equal Opportunity and Attorney General Nicholas Katzenbach. He stressed that all citizens, not just white citizens, should be free to exercise their right to vote without harassment, police brutality, and economic intimidation.

A subsequent movement was launched by the Congress of Racial Equality (CORE). A Freedom Ride Coordinating Committee was formed with King as Chairman to expand the sit-in protests to interstate buses. Pairs of blacks and whites boarded buses in the South to test compliance with the new federal law forbidding segregated accommodations in bus stations. This led to violence by whites who overturned and burned buses, assaulted the

Freedom Riders and attacked media reporters. Many arrested riders went to prison rather than pay fines. However, the Freedom Rider protests eventually led to the Interstate Commerce Committee enforcing non-segregation laws on interstate buses and their terminals.

Birmingham, Alabama was considered the most segregated city in the United States. King therefore led a campaign to desegregate Birmingham restaurants, hotels, department stores, rest rooms, and public facilities. The Birmingham Campaign by King and the SCLC was pivotal for the civil rights movement. For more than two months there were nonviolent protests against discriminatory economic and human civil rights. Businesses which did not offer racial equality for job opportunities were boycotted. The sit-ins and marches were undertaken with the goal that protestors would be arrested and thereby filling the jails. With the mass arrest of adult protestors a Children's Crusade occurred in which children also began to protest. Eugene "Bull" Connor-led police used clubs and dogs, while firemen used high pressure water jets against the protestors. Sometimes the power of the water hoses was strong enough to tear the bark off of trees. These cruel acts were widely publicized nationally by the press. Over 1000 grade school and high school children were jailed alongside adults. There was a total of over 3000 protestors arrested. A church was bombed and four girls attending Sunday

School were killed. Ku Klux Klan members bombed the home of King's brother, Reverend A.D. King, and the Gaston Motel where SCLC members were headquartered. Enraged blacks rioted and Alabama troopers set up undeclared martial law. The state court issued an injunction to bar further protests. King and Abernathy defied the court order, were arrested and placed in solitary confinement. Coretta King, who had just delivered their fourth child, Bernice, and therefore was not with King in Birmingham. She had always been with Martin to provide strength and faith at times of adversity, such as in Montgomery and Albany. She remembered JFK's call to her previously when Martin had been jailed in Atlanta. So Coretta called Robert Kennedy, then President Kennedy returned her call and King was removed from solitary confinement. Even more important, Harry Belafonte had raised $50,000 to provide bail for the three hundred arrested protesters including King and Abernathy. It was in jail that King, who was being criticized by white clergy, wrote his famous "Letter from

King in Birmingham jail

Birmingham City Jail." The clergy had written in a newspaper that the time for protests was not right; the protesters must have the patience to wait. In his letter of response King wrote:

> Perhaps it is easy for those who have never felt the stinging darts of segregation to say, "Wait." But when you have seen vicious mobs lynch your mothers and fathers at whim; when you have seen hate-filled policemen curse, kick, and even kill your black brothers and sisters; when you see the vast majority of your twenty million Negro brothers smothering in an airtight cage of poverty in the midst of an affluent society; when you suddenly find your tongue twisted and your speech stammering as you seek to explain to your six-year-old daughter why she can't go to the public amusement park that has just been advertised on television, and see tears welling up in her eyes when she is told that Funtown is closed to colored children, and see ominous clouds of inferiority beginning to form in her little mental sky, and see her beginning to distort her personality by developing an unconscious bitterness toward white people, when you have to concoct an answer for a five-year-old son who is asking: "Daddy, why do white people treat colored people so mean?"; when you take a cross-country drive and find it necessary to sleep night after night in the uncomfortable corners of your automobile because no motel will accept you; when you are humiliated day in and day out by nagging signs reading "white" and "colored"; when your first names becomes "nigger," your middle names become "boy" (however old you are), and your last names become "John," and your wife and mother are never given the respected title "Mrs."; when you are harried by day and haunted by night by the fact that you are a Negro, living constantly at tiptoe stance, never quite knowing what to expect next, and are plagued with inner fears and outer resentments; when you are forever fighting a degenerating sense of "nobodiness" - then you will understand why we find it difficult to wait.

Some other excerpts are the following:

- "Injustice anywhere is a threat to justice everywhere. "

- "We will have to repent in this generation not merely for the hateful words and actions of the bad people but for the appalling silence of the good people."

- "I submit that an individual who breaks a law that conscience tells him is unjust, and willingly accepts the penalty by staying in jail in order to arouse the conscience of the community over its injustice, is in reality expressing the very highest respect for the law."

- "Any law that degrades human personality is unjust."

King speaking at the March on Washington

President Kennedy was outraged with the violence against protesters in Birmingham. He ordered 3000 federal troops into protests around Birmingham. This stopped the violence. Ultimately Connor was removed and public places in Birmingham became more open to blacks. A committee of 125 Birmingham business leaders agreed to desegregation of lunch counters, rest rooms, and drinking fountains. Upgrading and hiring Negroes on a nondiscriminatory basis was included in the agreement.

One hundred years after the Emancipation Proclamation by Abraham Lincoln, the March on Washington for Jobs and Freedom occurred on August 28, 1963. The sponsoring leaders were: King for the SCLC; Roy Wilkens for the National Association of Colored People; Whitney Young, National Urban League; A. Phillip Randolph, Brotherhood for Sleeping Car Porters; John

Lewis, SNCC; and James L. Farmer, Jr, Congress of Racial Equality. President John F. Kennedy was worried that this March would have a negative effect on the passage of civil rights legislation. King acquiesced to Kennedy's concern and the March took on a less aggressive tone for which he was criticized by his colleagues. Malcolm X called the March a "Farce on Washington" and the Nation Islam forbid their members from participating. Important demands, however, were achieved eventually, including ending racial segregation in public schools, enacting civil rights legislation, protecting civil rights workers from police brutality, and a $2 minimum wage passed for all workers. A quarter million attended the Jobs and Freedom March and the marchers stretched from the Lincoln Memorial on to the National Mall and around the reflecting pool. This was the largest group of protestors ever in Washington D.C.

King's "I Have a Dream" speech on the steps of the Lincoln Memorial was the highlight of the Washington D.C. March. He said, "I have dream that one day on the red hills of Georgia the sons of former slaves and the sons of former slave owners will be able to sit down at the table of brotherhood." "I have a dream that my four little children will one day live in a nation where they will not be judged by the color of their skin but by the content of their character."

King went on to say, "When we let freedom ring, when we let it ring from every tenement and every hamlet, from every state and every city, we will be able to speed up that day when all of God's children, black men and white

*The March on Washington (left) and
King delivering the "I Have a Dream" speech (right)*

men, Jews and Gentiles, Protestants and Catholics, will be able to join hands and sing in the words of the old spiritual, 'Free at last, free at last. Thank God Almighty, we are free at last.' "King's speech had a positive impact on the passage of the Civil Rights Act in 1964 during the Lyndon Johnson presidency. The tragic assassination of Kennedy also created a climate for

King with President Johnson

passage of the laws. This hallmark legislation, along with the Voting Rights Act in 1965, supported desegregation, equal labor rights, the right to vote and other basic civil rights for equality independent of race or ethnicity. This included equal access for all US citizens to public accommodations, employment and education. The Voting Rights Act ended literacy tests and poll taxes as laws necessary for citizens to vote. All elections also were allowed to be investigated for their fairness.

In Selma, Alabama the Student Nonviolent Coordinating Committee (SNCC) was working for voter registration until a local judge barred a gathering of three or more people under the sponsorship of SCLC or SNCC. The civil rights activities then stopped until King defied the judge's injunction by speaking to a group in the Brown Chapel. King was jailed with 200 others after a voters' rights march in Selma. After so many years of intimidation only 350 of 15,000 Negroes in Selma and the surrounding Dallas County were registered to vote. The struggle for equal voting rights continued with the nonviolent march from Selma, Alabama to the state capitol in Montgomery. The first day of the march, March 7, 1965, has been termed "Blood Sunday" because of mob and police violence against the marchers. It was in Selma that a white woman, Viola Luizzo, was murdered by the Ku Klux Klan for standing up for Negro rights. It was in Selma where the white Reverend James Reeb died after beaten by white racists. Governor George Wallace refused permission for the march and the approximate 500 protestors who had gathered for the march were beaten and tear-gassed. Media footage of the brutality to the marchers received national coverage and resulted in public outrage. On March 9, 1965 King attempted another march to Montgomery which a judge ruled against. Nevertheless King led a march to the Pettus Bridge in Selma, which was blocked shoulder to shoulder by state troopers.

He held a prayer meeting there and then dispersed the marchers to avoid violence. Finally on the third try with intervention by federal troops and the National Guard 300 marchers were allowed to make

1965

the 4 day march from Selma to Montgomery. The marchers were joined in Montgomery by 50,000 nonviolent protestors and a petition for racial equality was delivered to Governor Wallace. On March 25, 1965, on the steps of the state capital King gave his "How Long, Not Long" speech. Here are excerpts from his speech.

> "How long will prejudice blind the visions of men, darken their understanding, and drive bright-eyed wisdom from her sacred throne?" "When will wounded justice, lying prostate on the streets of Selma and Birmingham and communities all over the South, be lifted from this dust of shame to reign supreme among the children of men?" "When will the radiant star of hope be plunged against the nocturnal bosom of the lonely night, plucked from weary souls with chains of fear and the manacles of death? How long will justice be crucified and truth beat it?" "How long? Not long because no lie can live forever." "How long? Not long because you still reap what you sow." "How long, not long because the arc of the moral universe is long, but it bends towards justice."

Medgar Wiley Evers

King was discouraged from visiting Mississippi where the NACCP representative, Medgar Evers, had been killed. Mississippi was considered a state where Negroes had suffered brutally from the police and killed by white mobs. King was told that there was a plot to kill him if he went to Mississippi. He, nevertheless, felt that he could not be effective in his civil rights struggle if the threat of harm or death inhibited him. King therefore traveled around the state of Mississippi and spoke in numerous cities and villages about the civil rights struggle for freedoms. To prevent Negroes from voting there was constant intimidation including violence and economic reprisals.

A highlight of King's leadership in civil rights was his being honored as the recipient of the Nobel Peace Prize on December 10, 1964. On the same day in Mississippi a U.S. Commissioner dismissed charges against nineteen white men who had been arrested by the FBI for the brutal killing of civil rights workers protesting for Negro voter rights registration.

In 1966 King and Abernathy moved into a slum area in Chicago to show support for the poor and to spread the civil rights movement to the North. The Chicago Freedom Movement was formed by the SCLC and the Coordinating Council of Community Organizations. They uncovered racially selective prejudice among housing requests even when income, background, number of children, and other factors were identical between whites and blacks. Blacks were shown primarily black areas and whites were shown primarily white areas. Abernathy wrote that in Chicago the SCLC received a worst reception than in the South. Bottles were thrown at them and mobs screamed epitaphs at them. In one march King was hit with a brick. After King returned to the South, Jesse Jackson, a seminary student, continued the struggle in Chicago. He organized Operation Breadbasket which targeted chain stores which were not treating blacks fairly.

King then broadened his civil rights struggle to include a peace movement. He opposed the Viet Nam War both on moral and economic grounds. He spoke out strongly stating that the U.S. government was trying to make Viet Nam an American colony. The U.S. government, however, stated that this was about the fight against Communism so as to avoid a domino effect of Communism in Southern Asia. The domino theory indicated that if Viet Nam was lost to Communism then many other countries in Southeast Asia would follow. This, fortunately, did not occur.

King also opposed the Viet Nam War on economic grounds. He felt the money and resources used to pursue the war in Viet Nam would have been better spent on the War on Poverty. He said, "A nation that continues year after year to spend more money on military defense than on programs of social uplift is approaching spiritual death." In contrast to King's support for the civil rights struggle, his Viet Nam stance lost him a lot of support from previous allies including President Lyndon Johnson, union leaders and the press. The Washington Post said that King had diminished his usefulness to the civil rights movement and to his country. While King was against unfettered capitalism which led to racial and economic injustice and disparities, he opposed Communism for its political totalitarianism and materialistic interpretation of history which rejected religion and supported atheism. King's attempt to develop a coalition between the peace and civil rights movements was of limited success. King nevertheless felt that there was an irony that blacks and whites were fighting and dying together in Viet Nam, yet they could not attend the same schools together in their own country.

In 1968 King and the SCLC organized the "Poor People's Campaign" which included a march on Washington D.C. to demand economic aid to the poorest communities throughout the country. There were those who felt the goal of the march was too diffuse and would lead to a backlash against blacks and the poor. There were also militant groups who were against King's nonviolent approach. This included Malcolm X and Nation of Islam. Stokely Carmichael, head of the SNCC,

King with Malcolm X (left); Stokely Carmichael (right)

espoused Black Power and black separatism in contrast to King's pleas for integration of the races.

On March 29, 1968 King went to Memphis, Tennessee to support black sanitation workers who had been on strike since March 12 for fair wages and improved working conditions. One example of injustice was when blacks and whites were sent home 2 hours after arriving because of bad weather. The white workers received a whole day's pay and the black workers received 2 hours pay. In Memphis, King gave his last speech before his assassination, "I Have Been to the Mountaintop." He had arrived late because of a bomb threat against his plane. King said, "I would like to live a long life ... but I am not concerned about that now. I just want to do God's will. And life's allowed me to go up to the mountain. And I have looked over. And I have seen the promised land. I may not get there with you. But I want you to know tonight, that we, as a people, will get to the Promised Land. And I'm happy, tonight. I'm not worried about anything. I'm not fearing any man. Mine eyes have seen the glory of the coming of the Lord."

King and his team stayed in room 306 at the Lorraine Motel in Memphis. They had stayed there so often that it was known as the King-Abernathy suite. King was standing on the motel's second floor balcony when he was shot at 6:01 pm on April 4, 1968. He underwent emergency chest surgery but was pronounced dead at St. Joseph's Hospital at 7:05 pm. The autopsy of the 39 year old King revealed a heart of a 60 year old man, perhaps related in part to the stress of his 13 years of civil rights struggles.

The assassination of Martin Luther King Jr. led to nationwide riots in numerous cities around the country in spite of pleas from Bobby Kennedy and others. President Johnson declared April 7 a national day of mourning. At Coretta King's request King's last "Drum Major" sermon at Ebenezer Baptist Church was played at his funeral. In that sermon, King asked that his awards and honors not be mentioned. Rather he said that he tried "to feed the hungry," "clothe the naked," "be right on the (Viet Nam) war question," and "love and serve humanity." Take My Hand, Precious Lord, was sung by Mahalia Jackson at the funeral. The sanitation workers strike was quickly settled in their favor.

The Lorraine Motel

Two months after Kings' murder, James Earl Ray was arrested at London Heathrow Airport on his way to white-ruled Rhodesia with a false Canadian passport in the name of Ramon George Sneyd. He was extradited to Tennessee, confessed and then recanted his confession of King's murder. He was convicted and sentenced to 99 years in jail. Ray was a thief and burglar, but had no record of violent crimes. There have been considerable conspiracy claims that Ray did not act alone. There was a conspiracy trial with a jury of 6 whites and 6 blacks which prosecuted Loyd Jowers, who claimed to have received $100,000 from the Mafia for arranging the King assassination. The King family won a wrongful death claim when Jowers was found guilty. The jury also ruled that governmental agencies were a party to the King assassination. In essence, King's lawyer, William P. Pepper, claimed that the government had been involved in the King assassination. The Justice Department did an extensive 18 month investigation, however, and their findings did not support Pepper's claims of government conspiracy in the assassination. James Bevel, King's friend, said that he would never believe that Ray, "a ten cent white boy," had the money, mobility and ability to escape unaided from Memphis, to Canada, to London without support.

When Hoover extended Kennedy's limited wiretapping of King's phones, the FBI began tapping King's phones in his home, office and even his hotel rooms when he was on the road. Although never proven, Hoover always believed that King had relationships with Communists. The wiretapping did lead to adultery allegations against King which were used to publicly denigrate him. The FBI claimed that King had numerous extramarital affairs. Lyndon Johnson once called King a hypocritical preacher. In his 1989 autobiography Abernathy wrote that King was a womanizer who had a weakness for women. David Garrow, who was King's biographer, also wrote about King's extramarital affairs. He claimed that one woman, whom King saw almost daily, became the centerpiece of King's extramarital life. Garrow felt that King's promiscuity caused him a great deal of emotional pain and guilt. The FBI distributed their reports about King's affair to reporters, SCLC funding supporters, his family and members of the government executive branch. They also sent anonymous letters to King threatening to publically reveal his extramarital affairs unless he stopped his civil rights activities. King did not yield to the FBI threats and continued his fight against racial inequality. The United States District Court has ordered all audiotapes and written transcripts from the FBI's electronic surveillance to be held in the National Archives without public access until 2027.

King with fellow civil rights leaders

Martin Luther King Jr. and his wife, Coretta Scott King

Martin Luther King Jr. was a man of great personal and moral courage whose legacy in the civil rights movement in the United States is unparalleled. He also had an influence on international racial affairs. His work was an inspiration to Albert Luthuli and Nelson Mandela, two winners of the Nobel Peace Prize for their fight against racial injustice in South Africa. For his nonviolent fight against racial injustice King received numerous awards. In 1964 he received the Nobel Peace Prize for his civil rights work. At 34 years of age King was the youngest recipient of the Nobel Peace Prize. In 1965 King received the American Liberties Medallion from the American Jewish Committee for his exceptional advancement of human liberties. Posthumously King received the Presidential Medal of

Martin Luther King Jr. Memorial

Freedom. Among his many other honors and awards were at least 50 honorary degrees from various universities. His wife, Coretta Scott King, established the King Center in Atlanta, Georgia which is dedicated to nonviolent conflict resolution and tolerance around the world. She was active in the fight for social justice and civil rights until her death in 2006. Coretta and King were awarded the Congressional Gold Medal in 2004 for their contributions to civil rights and justice equality. There are 730 U.S. cities who have streets named after Marin Luther King Jr. The Gallup Poll listed King as one of the most admired people in the 20th Century. In 1963 King was named "Man of the Year" by Time Magazine, the first black man to be so honored. The third Monday in January every year has been designated as Martin Luther King Sr. National holiday. The Martin Luther King Jr. Memorial along the Tidal Basin at the National Mall in Washington D.C. is the only memorial there to honor an individual who had not been president of the United States. King said, "The quality, not the longevity, of one's life is what is important." Certainly his early death at age 39 and his contributions to making our nation more just and free is a testimony to this quote. He also said, "No, no, we are not satisfied until justice rolls down like the waters and righteousness like a mighty stream."

"Every now and then I think about my own death and "What is it that I would want said?"

- I'd like somebody to mention that day that Martin Luther King, Jr., tried to give his life serving others.

- I'd like for somebody to say that day that Martin Luther King, Jr., tried to love somebody.

- I want you to say that day that I tried to be right on the war question.

- I want you to be able to say that day that I did try to feed the hungry.

- And I want you to be able to say that day that I did try in my life to clothe those who were naked.

- I want you to say on that day that I did try in my life to visit those who were in prison.

- I want you to say that I tried to love and serve humanity.

"Yes, if you want to say that I was a drum major, say that I was a drum major for justice. Say that I was a drum major for peace. I was a drum major for righteousness. And all of the other shallow things will not matter. I won't have any money to leave behind. I won't have the fine and luxurious things of life to leave behind. But I just want to leave a committed life behind. And that's all I want to say."

"If I can help somebody as I pass along, if I can cheer somebody with a word or song, if I can show somebody he's traveling wrong, then my living will not be in vain. If I can do my duty as a Christian ought, if I can bring salvation to a world once wrought, if I can spread the message as the master taught, then my living will not be in vain."

Abraham Lincoln

- Pictures from "Looking for Lincoln: The Making of an American Icon," by Philip B. Kunhardt III, Peter W. Kunhardt, and Peter W. Kunhardt, Jr. Alfred A. Knopf, New York 2008.

- Baker, Jean H. (1989). *Mary Todd Lincoln: A Biography*. W. W. Norton & Company. ISBN 9780393305869.
- Donald, David Herbert (2001). *Lincoln Reconsidered*. Knopf Doubleday Publishing Group. ISBN 9780375725326.
- Goodwin, Doris Kearns (2005). *Team of Rivals: The Political Genius of Abraham Lincoln*. Simon & Schuster. ISBN 0684824906.
- Goodrich, Thomas (2005). *The Darkest Dawn: Lincoln, Booth, and the Great American Tragedy*. Indiana University Press.ISBN 9780253345677.
- Harris, William C. (2007). *Lincoln's Rise to the Presidency*. University Press of Kansas. ISBN 9780700615209.
- Keckley, Elizabeth (2011). *Behind the Scenes: Or, Thirty years a slave, and Four Years in the White House*. ISBN 1605209309.
- McPherson, James M. (2009). *Abraham Lincoln*. Oxford University Press. ISBN 9780195374520.
- Neely, Mark E (1994). *The Last Best Hope of Earth: Abraham Lincoln and the Promise of America*. Harvard University Press.ISBN 9780674511255.
- Peterson, Merrill D. (1995). *Lincoln in American Memory*. Oxford University Press. ISBN 9780195096453.
- Schwartz, Barry (2000). *Abraham Lincoln and the Forge of National Memory*. University Of Chicago Press. ISBN 978-0226741970.

Mahatma Gandhi

- Gandhi, M.K. *The Gandhi Reader: A Sourcebook of His Life and Writings*. Homer Jack (ed.) Grove Press, New York, 1956.
- Gandhi, M.K. (1940). *An Autobiography or The Story of My Experiments With Truth* (2 ed.). Ahmedabad: Navajivan Publishing House. pp. xii, 404. ISBN 0-8070-5909-9. Also available at Wikisource.
- Bhana, Surendra and Goolam Vahed. *The Making of a Political Reformer: Gandhi in South Africa, 1893–1914*. New Delhi: Manohar, 2005.

- Brown, Judith M. *Gandhi: Prisoner of Hope* (1991); 456pp; a major scholarly biography
- Brown, Judith M., and Anthony Parel, eds. *The Cambridge Companion to Gandhi* (Cambridge Companions to Religion) (2011), advanced essays by scholars excerpt and text search
- Chadha, Yogesh. *Gandhi: A Life.* ISBN 0-471-35062-1
- Easwaran, Eknath. *Gandhi the Man.* ISBN 978-1586380557 ebook: ISBN 978-1586380670
- Fischer, Louis. *The Life of Mahatma Gandhi.* Harper & Row, New York, 1950. ISBB 0-06-091038-0 (1983 pbk.)
- Gandhi, Rajmohan (2007). *Gandhi: the man, his people, and the empire.* University of California Press, 2008. ISBN 0520255704, 9780520255708.
- Hardiman, David. *Gandhi in His Time and Ours: The Global Legacy of His Ideas* (2003), 256pp
- Herman, Arthur. *Gandhi and Churchill: The Epic Rivalry that Destroyed an Empire and Forged Our Age* (2009)
- Lelyveld, Joseph. *Great Soul: Mahatma Gandhi and His Struggle with India* (2011), 448pp; a major scholarly biography excerpt and text search
- Sofri, Gianni. *Gandhi and India: A Century in Focus.* (1995) ISBN 1-900624-12-5

Nelson Mandela

- *A Prisoner in the Garden: Opening Nelson Mandela's Prison Archive.* Penguin Books. 2005. ISBN 0-143-02495-7.
- Benson, Mary. *Nelson Mandela: The Man and the Movement.*
- Bezdrob, Anne Marie du Preez (2006). *The Nelson Mandela Story.* Samoja Books. ISBN 0-620-36570-6.
- Cohen, David Elliott. (2009). *Nelson Mandela: A Life in Photographs.* Sterling Publishing. ISBN 978-1-4027-7707-3.
- Denenberg, Barry. *Nelson Mandela: No Easy Walk To Freedom.*
- Hoobler, Dorothy; Hoobler, Thomas (1992). *Mandela: The Man, The Struggle, The Triumph.* New York: Franklin Watts. ISBN 978-0531152454.
- Maharaj, Mac; Kathrada, Ahmed. *Mandela: The Authorized Portrait.* Andrews McMeel Publishing. ISBN 978-0-7407-5572-9.
- Mandela, Nelson (2010). *Conversations with Myself.* Macmillan. ISBN 978-0-230-74901-6.

- Mandela, Nelson (1995). *Long Walk to Freedom*. Little, Brown and Company. ISBN 0-316-54818-9.
- Sampson, Anthony (1999). *Mandela: The Authorised Biography*. New York: Vintage Books. ISBN 0-679-78178-1.
- Villa-Vicencio, Charles (1996). *The Spirit of Freedom*. Berkeley: University of California Press.

Martin Luther King Jr.

- Abernathy, Ralph (1989). *And the Walls Came Tumbling Down: An Autobiography*. Harper & Row. ISBN 0060161922.
- Ayton, Mel (2005). *A Racial Crime: James Earl Ray And The Murder Of Martin Luther King Jr*. Archebooks Publishing. ISBN 1595070753.
- Branch, Taylor (1988). *Parting the Waters: America in the King Years, 1954–1963*. Simon & Schuster. ISBN 0671460978.
- Branch, Taylor (1998). *Pillar of Fire: America in the King Years, 1963–1965*. Simon & Schuster. ISBN 0684808196.
- Branch, Taylor (2006). *At Canaan's Edge: America In the King Years, 1965–1968*. Simon & Schuster. ISBN 068485712X.
- Jackson, Thomas F. (2006). *From Civil Rights to Human Rights: Martin Luther King, Jr., and the Struggle for Economic Justice*. University of Pennsylvania Press. ISBN 9780812239690.
- King, Coretta Scott (1993) [1969]. *My Life with Martin Luther King, Jr*. Henry Holth & Co. ISBN 080502445X.
- Kirk, John A. (2005). *Martin Luther King, Jr*. Pearson Longman. ISBN 0582414318.
- Carson, Clayborne. "Mythology and the Charismatic Leadership of Martin Luther King". In Gerster, Patrick; Cords, Nicholas. *Myth America: A Historical Anthology, Volume II*. St. James, NY: Brandywine Press. (1997). ISBN 978-1-881089-97-1
- Garrow, David. *Bearing the Cross: Martin Luther King, Jr., and the Southern Christian Leadership Conference* (1989). Pulitzer Prize. ISBN 978-0-06-056692-0
- Kirk, John A., ed. *Martin Luther King Jr. and the Civil Rights Movement: Controversies and Debates* (2007). 224 pp.
- Schulke, Flip; McPhee, Penelope. *King Remembered*, Foreword by Jesse Jackson (1986). ISBN 978-1-4039-9654-1
- Kotz, Nick, *Judgment Days: Lyndon Baines Johnson, Martin Luther King Jr., and the Laws that Changed America* (2005). ISBN 978-0-618-64183-3

Printed in Great Britain
by Amazon